Profitable
Woodworking

Profitable Woodworking

Turning Your Hobby into a Profession

Martin Edic

The Taunton Press

Taunton
BOOKS & VIDEOS
for fellow enthusiasts

First printing: 1996
Printed in the United States of America

A Fine Woodworking Book
Fine Woodworking® is a trademark of The Taunton Press, Inc.,
registered in the U.S. Patent and Trademark Office.

The Taunton Press, 63 South Main Street, Box 5506,
Newtown, CT 06470-5506

Library of Congress Cataloging-in-Publication Data

Edic, Martin.
    Profitable woodworking : turning your hobby into a profession /
Martin Edic.
        p.   cm.
    "A Fine woodworking book."
    Includes index.
    ISBN 1-56158-122-4
    1. Woodworking industries—Management. 2. New business
enterprises—Management. 3. Woodwork—Marketing. I. Title.
HD9773.A2E338   1996
684'.08'068—dc20   96-21057
                                                         CIP

ACKNOWLEDGMENTS

Thanks to the many woodworkers who shook their heads when asked about the woodworking business and then proceeded to offer valued and realistic information for new shop owners.

INTRODUCTION

The "profit" in this book's title is more than the dollars and cents remaining after the bills are paid. In being a woodworker, you've chosen a rewarding profession or hobby that satisfies you on many levels, including the satisfaction that comes from making something with your hands. When you go into business for yourself, many of the profits are psychological, such as the sense of liberation that comes with being your own boss, the realization of what is truly "the American dream" (and increasingly a global one) and the respect you receive from others for being a self-made person.

The downside of this vision of financial and personal prosperity is the disturbing dose of reality involved in running a successful business. There is as much or more skill involved in being an entrepreneur as there is in learning your craft. Typically woodworkers build their skills as hobbyists, students or helpers and then decide to use those skills to make a living. However, they soon discover that starting a business is more complicated than they'd imagined. Not only complicated, but downright scary as bills pile up and work fails to materialize. When this happens the entrepreneur is faced with two choices: Go out of business or learn new skills to make it possible to succeed in the business. I wrote this book to help those who are starting woodworking businesses or contemplating doing so.

As I said in my previous book, *The Woodworker's Marketing Guide,* I believe that success comes from careful planning and a willingness to remain open-minded about a business. Woodworking is an area that encompasses everything from handmade clock cases to industrial prototypes, and its practitioners range from operators of computer-controlled machinery to the solitary carver working in the corner of his or her basement. My focus in *Profitable Woodworking* is the small shop with an owner-operator and few or no employees. I believe, however, that the information offered here will be useful to larger companies and hobbyists seeking to earn part-time income from their work as well.

The best advice I can give to any business owner is that experience is enhanced through constant learning and adaptation. The real profits of owning a shop are the day-to-day challenges you face and how they affect your life. We can set goals for income or retirement, but it is how we pursue these goals that ultimately defines the purpose of our lives. It is my hope that the information and profiles from woodworking entrepreneurs in this book will enhance that valuable experience for you.

ABOUT THE PROFILES

I've included a half dozen profiles in the book, representing a cross section of woodworkers and woodworking-related experiences. If you pick up any telephone book and look under Woodworking in the Yellow Pages, you'll find a similar selection. I wanted to capture the experience of performing the work and being involved in the business of woodworking with regular people who are doing it daily. Once you are buying materials, taking classes or running your shop, you'll meet people just like the ones I talked to for these profiles. Ask them about their experiences. Pick their brains and share information. You'll find new customers, learn new skills, avoid mistakes and have a good time talking shop. And you'll find yourself accepted as one of a hardworking club: Those who successfully pursue the profession of woodworking.

CONTENTS

CAN I MAKE A LIVING AS A WOODWORKER?

Whether or not they can make a living as woodworkers is the question many amateurs ask themselves at one point or another. Answering that question and the others that follow is the goal of this book. The dream of making your living as a craftsperson is enticing, conjuring up images of being a skilled artisan creating beautiful and useful things from wood, all the while earning a good living. You may imagine a large shop filled with professional tools or simply be interested in having a special interest and making a little money on the side. Whether you aspire to ownership of a growing business or just want to develop a part-time income doing something you love, you'll be facing the same decision-making process.

Profitable Woodworking will guide you through the process of setting up and successfully running a woodworking business. Much of what is discussed here represents the nuts-and-bolts, real-world skill of being a business owner. As a marketing consultant specializing in new businesses and having a special soft spot for woodworkers, I've found that these basic business skills are often what stands between the successful and the unsuccessful craftsperson. Success in business is measured by several criteria, including profit, growth and personal satisfaction. Because you cannot have growth and satisfaction without at least a minimal profit, my emphasis is on getting your woodworking business going and making it profitable as soon as possible.

In this chapter we're going to look at different kinds of woodshops and answer some of the most common questions: How much money can I make? How much money will I need to get started? How hard will it be to succeed?

A SAMPLING OF WOODWORKING BUSINESSES

We start with a quick overview of what kinds of businesses qualify as woodworking businesses. Wood is a universal material found nearly everywhere on earth and in use by humans for all of recorded history. It has so many uses that a business called a woodworking business can be anything from a custom furnituremaker to a factory turning out thousands of identical toothpicks made of wood. A woodworking business can generate great art or strictly utilitarian fare. A craftsman might make his living making chin rests for violins, the violins themselves, music stands, instrument cases, the casework for a theater or the walnut burl dashboards of the cars music lovers drive to a concert. Woodworkers make the cabinetry used in recording studios to hold audio equipment, the shelves for your CD collection and the chair in which you relax while listening.

THE VALUE OF SPECIALIZATION

These examples of the variety of woodworking in the music world have something in common: Each is a specialization, whether the specialization is skill based (carving, cabinetmaking, finishing, etc.) or product based (chin rests, instruments, mass-production components, architectural products, etc.). In business, this is known as a vertical market because most of these products belong to a specific niche, music, rather than a general category, or horizontal market, such as cabinetry or furnituremaking. Why is this important?

To put it simply, it is easier to find buyers for a specialized product. If you are a specialist, you know what your market wants and how to find your market. You also have the opportunity to develop highly specialized skills that command higher prices. Choosing a specialty or working a vertical market rather than in a broad one is an excellent strategy for starting a business. Many of the woodworkers I profile in this book started out as hobbyists or knowledgeable consumers who recognized a need and started their woodworking business to fulfill that need.

Even the general-interest woodworker usually specializes in some aspect of woodworking based on a particular set of skills. Veneering, bending or laminating wood requires different skills and tools from cabinetmaking or woodturning. These horizontal-market woodshops still specialize and can take advantage of specialization to achieve success. We'll be looking at examples of these kinds of businesses too.

Let's start with a woodworking business whose products are things with which most of us are familiar: the crafts business.

▼▼▼

CRAFTING A LIVING

The woodworking crafts business includes many kinds of products and woodworkers. One craftsperson might make small inexpensive gift items such as cutting boards or birdhouses, while another may build and sell a line of furniture. From a business perspective, the common denominator is a product line that retails or wholesales through outlets such as craft shows, arts festivals, gift shops and craft galleries. Creating and building a product line for these outlets is different from building custom furniture or creating fine arts. At the highest skill level and price range, the differences between fine furniture and craft work begin to blur. Indeed, many craft galleries combine the functions of art gallery and retail outlet.

Many craft woodworkers operate on a yearly or seasonal schedule. If they sell primarily through festivals and shows, they base their schedule on the deadlines and dates for those shows. If they exhibit and sell through established retail outlets such as gift shops and craft galleries, they usually spend the entire year preparing for the Christmas buying season. If they also market their wares in resort areas, the peak tourist season will influence their deadlines. Buyers are usually making their Christmas buying decisions in February or March. The seasonal nature of the craft woodworker's market is one of the reasons he or she must produce pieces in quantity rather than making individual pieces based on an individual buyer's desires. If you are selling 90% of your work in one month of the year, which is not uncommon, you'll have to produce a large quantity of goods or inventory in order to be prepared for the busy season.

There is an element of risk in the crafts business, particularly at the beginning. You may spend several months designing and building hundreds of items and then have the buying public give your work the thumbs-down sign. It is vital in the crafts business to be responsive to what the market is interested in, to stay aware of trends and to plan your product based on the results of your inquiries rather than on what interests you.

Craft woodworking businesses can be small shops or factories. If at some point the scale becomes too large, the items produced will no longer be considered handcrafted, and the product line will be geared to the mass market. If this kind of operation is your goal, you'll be spending more time with management, manufacturing and sales than woodworking. Mass-market production lines require mass markets, and such businesses do most of their selling to buyers at trade shows. They also face intense competition from factories overseas. It's a tough business.

In this book, we'll be looking at the smaller craft-oriented business based around the work of an individual craftsperson or small shop. These businesses often specialize in a particular line and style and build up business by personally selling their product directly to the public at shows or to buyers from galleries and gift shops. They have their own craft-related trade shows where they can show their wares and take orders. Once they have an idea of where they'll be selling and what kind of volume they can expect, they plan their production and spend several months (often during the winter) building an inventory. It can be a lucrative, interesting life, especially if you enjoy sales, travel and meeting the public. We'll take an in-depth look at the crafts business in Chapters 11 and 12.

▼▼▼

THE SPECIALIST CRAFTSPERSON

In the woodworking world, another way to specialize is to develop a particular skill to the point where it becomes art. This kind of woodworker is often very specialized, creates one-of-a-kind items and develops a reputation among aficionados of that specialty. A good example is the professional woodturner who creates unique bowls and sculptural wood objects from unusual woods, including burls and other highly figured or uncommonly shaped wood. Usually working out of a small shop, either alone or with assistants who serve an apprentice role, these artists build creative reputations through coverage in publications, gallery representation and informal word of mouth among collectors. Often their pieces sell for significant amounts of money, and if they are skilled enough, there may be a waiting list for their work.

These artist/craftspeople may sell their work through some of the same outlets as the craft woodworkers we looked at earlier; however, they don't do production work, and their designs are characterized by personal vision and creativity. Their reputations as fine artists create their market. Their marketing, business calendar and day-to-day work life is different from that of the production craftsperson. We'll look at how to break into fine-arts woodworking in Chapter 14.

THE FURNITUREMAKER

The average person usually imagines that a woodworker is a skilled person who works in a dusty shop building furniture, and with good reason. Furniture is our most tangible contact with wood. We grew up with pieces that became heirlooms, we come in contact with wood furniture every day, and we fill our homes with it if we can afford it. Most people probably don't know that the furniture they see, including their beloved antiques, was made in factories. In fact, furnituremaking was one of the first crafts to be automated, with the coming of the Industrial Revolution. Mass-produced furniture became a common part of our lives. At the same time, custom-made or one-of-a-kind furniture became luxurious items. This has been both good and bad for custom woodworkers.

The custom furnituremaker builds one-of-a-kind or limited-edition furniture from the designs of others or from an original design—a significant difference from a business perspective. Most seem to do both because the market for custom-designed and fabricated furnishings is limited by price and the tendency of people to buy according to trends and styles. This is where custom furnituremaking is paradoxical. Often, fine furnituremakers will go to crafts schools or serve an apprenticeship to learn their craft. They then believe that appreciation for their skills will cause buyers to descend on them in droves, giving them substantial commissions from wealthy individuals, corporations and architects or designers. What they discover is that these markets are limited. So the custom furnituremaker turns to other kinds of work to pay the bills.

This work may include general woodworking tasks such as cabinetmaking or building pieces to the designs of others. If woodworkers are truly committed to custom furnituremaking, they usually work toward developing the gallery and media exposure required to build a reputation, while continuing to do commercial work to survive. While this scenario is one of the most common in the small-shop woodworking world, it doesn't hold much promise for success. The most successful shops are the ones where woodworker/owners invest as much energy in learning business skills as they apply to woodworking. Often, woodworkers avoid these real-world skills and then wonder why they aren't making a living.

THE CABINETMAKER

Besides furnituremaking, cabinetmaking is probably the largest woodworking niche business. Cabinetmaking in general is a horizontal business serving many segments of society, from homeowners remodeling their kitchens to corporate boardrooms filled with media walls and libraries. At the same time cabinetmaking can serve a vertical market specializing in a particular kind of cabinetry. This might include audiovisual cabinetry, kitchens, computer desks or cabinetry for retail stores. You can further specialize within an area. A good example might be the cabinetmaker who specializes in audiovisual cabinetry for professional recording studios and TV stations. Such a shop would know the language and specialized requirements of its market and could charge a premium for its expertise.

Cabinet shops can be small shops that build every component or larger facilities that outsource, buying components and assembling them into a "custom" product. Often, cabinet shops do both to increase their flexibility and profitability. Fabricating and selling cabinets demands different shop setups and planning and design skills from furnituremaking or woodworking crafts, and the market is considerably different.

The main difference in the market is that cabinets are found everywhere. Unlike fine furniture, cabinetry is found all around the average house or office, and in every store, restaurant and other public area. The market is enormous. However, the competition from major manufacturers, midsize local shops, local home centers, office-equipment retailers and dozens of other places is fierce. The consumer has many choices in regard to price and style. The small cabinet shop must find an edge to prosper in this highly competitive market.

The edge is usually related to quality, service and specialization. In order to compete, you must offer many solutions for your customers, find customers who understand the advantages of doing business with you and develop a marketing attitude that helps you to move with the trends. These characteristics are critical to the success of any woodworking business but become especially important when working in the highly competitive cabinet market.

THE ARTIST/WOODWORKER

Artists who choose to use wood as their principal medium are entirely different from other woodworkers. They are artists and visionaries first and craftspersons second. Because their work is driven by their inner vision and sells only because that vision resonates with a buyer, they face many different challenges. It might seem that being businesslike is not one of them; however, artists need to eat, like the rest of us. They cannot pursue their art without a means of support, whether that support comes from grants or sales, or a combination of the two. Artist/woodworkers have their own unique business challenges.

If you study the lives of famous artists of the last hundred years, you'll often find that they were relentless self-promoters and that they worked extremely hard every day, whether inspiration knocked or not. Painters such as Picasso and Jackson Pollock (to name two different examples) were conscious of their reputations, their gallery relationships, their fellow artists' work and the world where they lived and sold their work. Even a famously unsuccessful (in his lifetime!) artist such as Van Gogh constantly wrote letters to anyone he could appealing for support, gallery representation and recognition. In his case, his art was not of his time, but it wasn't long after his death before he was recognized for his genius. Today, in our information-driven world, it is less likely that an artist of his stature would remain undiscovered in his lifetime.

There is a business of fine art, and the artist/woodworker can profit from learning its ways. Galleries, grant makers, corporate supporters, museums and publications have means of connecting with the savvy artist. If you wish to pursue your artistic vision as a woodworker, you'd be well advised to learn the ropes of the world you need to enter to succeed. In Chapter 14 we'll look at the gateways to that world and the means to get your work seen.

These profiles of several popular kinds of professional woodworking are meant to serve as an overview of the craft. To prosper and profit as a professional woodworker, you must educate yourself, plan your entry and execute that plan step-by-step. The rewards can be both monetary and personal—you can earn a decent living and derive satisfaction from making objects that others value for utilitarian and aesthetic reasons.

Making the transition from hobbyist to professional is often difficult. I'd like to chart one possible route and offer some answers to the question I often hear: How much money can I expect to make?

▼▼▼

THE TRANSITION TO PROFESSIONALISM

A beginning interest in woodworking can lead one to becoming a professional craftsperson. You need to set goals, develop a simple plan and determine whether your plan is realistic before taking the plunge. Often someone will get a commission from a friend, relative or chance encounter and dive into business, purchasing tools and supplies and assuming that work will be relatively easy to get. A month or two later this person is out of work and facing the depressing conclusion that being a woodworker is harder than he or she thought. I'd like to offer an alternative to becoming a pro.

I recommend starting out slowly, choosing a niche based on your interests and what the market will pay for, and making a gradual transition from amateur to professional. In *Profitable Woodworking,* we'll start with the basics of being in business, we'll look at how to evaluate your strengths and weaknesses, and we'll learn how to find markets for your work. All of these basics are skills not unlike the woodworking skills you'll acquire over time. Skills are learned from doing, not from observing or reading. Because it takes time to learn business skills, I often look for ways people can start a new business gradually without taking a blind leap.

Starting gradually means keeping your day job or having a spouse with sufficient income to pay the bills. It might mean finding enough capital (money) to cover your living and business expenses for 6 to 12 months. Or it might mean starting out with a minibusiness run out of your home shop at night and on weekends, gradually building up your cash flow until you can justify going full time. This is probably the most realistic choice for new woodworkers just finding their way. You test the waters and consider the time involved as education that will help you develop the skills and knowledge to succeed. Some of you may find that the business is not for you. This can be an extremely valuable lesson to learn before you burn your bridges, quit your job or commit to an expensive loan and lease.

Throughout *Profitable Woodworking* you'll find interviews with established professional woodworkers of many kinds. The emphasis in the interviews is on how they started, the mistakes and successes they experienced and the lessons they learned. Their experiences can tell you a great deal about the business of woodworking and how your life would be if you became a pro.

▼▼▼

MONEY

As I mentioned earlier, people want to know if they can make money if they become self-employed woodworkers. It is for good reason that this book is called *Profitable Woodworking*. Without profits and cash flow, you cannot survive as a woodworker, and mere survival is not enough. I want to see you go beyond survival and make the living you want as a woodworker. We have a tendency to rise to the limits we set on ourselves. If you persist in seeing yourself as a humble craftsman scratching out a simple living, you will not reach much further than that. If making millions is your goal, your entire outlook will be different and you'll probably look upon a business such as woodworking as only one step along the way. If you believe that woodworkers must struggle, you will struggle. If you believe (as I do) that you pursue a highly skilled and honorable profession that can and should be profitable, then you will be. A good attitude is the key to success.

So how much? Let's look at a small shop specializing in audiovisual cabinetry and home-theater systems with an owner and one employee. The owner knows from his bookkeeping that it cost him $25/hour per man to pay his overhead and salaries. He adds on $10 to get a shop rate of $35/hour, which is the basis for the labor and overhead in his bids. The $10 is miscellaneous expenses and profit or markup. He bids a job by adding up the hours of time necessary for sales, construction, design, ordering and picking up materials, etc. Items that he outsources, such as hardware, electronics and manufactured components, are marked up to compensate for the time he spends finding them and to build in more profit. Materials are added in and he gets a figure. To this he adds profit. Then he considers the figure in light of his experience with the market or customer and decides if it's too low or too high, adjusting accordingly. If it's too high, he either finds places to lower his rates, cut time or do the job quicker or he passes on the bid. If it is too low, he marks it up and rechecks his figures.

After the job is finished and paid for, the money pays employees, overhead, his own salary and suppliers. Whatever is left is profit. This is used for capital investments on things such as tools or marketing, or he puts it in his pocket or both. So how much is it? In today's world the owner might put $17 in his pocket, pay his employee $12, and put $7 toward overhead and $4 for profit, adding up to gross income of $40. He makes between $17 and $21 dollars an hour if he stays busy.

These numbers vary but are a reasonable expectation for the woodworker with a few years of experience. The challenge is to stay busy and keep the work flowing to the market. Learning to generate and improve cash flow is vital to any business, small or large.

Those seeking millions from their skills had better start gearing up for a very different scenario, involving manufacturing, licensing of inventions or perhaps becoming a world-famous artist. These goals are beyond the scope of this book, although the strategies covered have been used by many start-up businesses to reach the big numbers. It could happen to you if you want it to.

CHAPTER 2

THE THINGS YOU MAKE AND SELL

Turning your personal interest into a business

A product line example

At a recent outdoor arts festival filled with the tents of hundreds of vendors, I noticed a lot of people carrying similar objects. On closer inspection, I saw that these objects were lawn ornaments made from a steel rod about 4 ft. long with a two-dimensional house made of wood on top. The brightly painted little house was about the size of a birdhouse, constructed with four pieces of wood nailed together and painted with folksy details such as window boxes. By the time I left the festival I'd seen dozens of these things, looked at the vendor's selection (at $18 each) and concluded that the object was an unlikely hit.

The process leading that craftsperson to that particular product design can only be surmised because the maker was unavailable, but my guess is that he or she started as a hobbyist and stuck a few ornaments in his yard, got requests from neighbors and passersby and discovered that he had stumbled upon a business. He probably spent the winter months putting these things together and applying to shows, then hit the road in the warmer months, selling several thousand dollars' worth each weekend from May to September. By the time the leaves began to fall he or she was back in the shop contemplating a successful season with $40,000 to $50,000 in the bank and wondering how to expand the line.

In case you think I'm suggesting you build lawn ornaments, let me assure you that this is just one example. Let's look at another situation. A woodworker starts developing his craft when he's young, eventually going to a famous school for craftspeople and learning from an acknowledged master craftsman. After school he joins the shop of the master and spends his days fabricating the master's one-of-a-kind designs for galleries and wealthy individuals, while working alongside other skilled woodworkers. They do quite well for several years as the master reaches the highest echelons of the art world, creating special pieces that are purchased by wealthy collectors and corporate art collections. Then the roaring eighties come to a screeching halt. The bottom falls out of the art market, and the master prudently decides to close his workshop and return to teaching and creating his own designs by himself. The dedicated and highly skilled woodworkers are laid off, and the master makes several calls informing other area shops of their availability. Our young craftsman is interviewed by one such shop.

After the interview the shop owner thanks him, praises his work and regrets to inform him that there is very little market for his skills, and if he's hired, he'll make much less money than he is used to and he'll be putting together cabinets and copies of Arts-and-Crafts furnishings. The young man declines the offer and decides to go into business for himself making the kind of furniture he loves. He borrows $50,000 from relatives and buys a shopful of equipment, signs a lease and has business cards printed. Then he sits in his shop and wonders where his business is, occasionally making a piece of furniture of his own design. A few galleries express interest in his work on a consignment basis, and he sends his portfolio to a number of architects and designers. One tells him that his work is wonderful but there are only so many millionaires buying furniture these days.

The moral of these two stories (and though they are both true, they have a fairy-tale quality) is that professionals must know their markets and work in accordance with them. As a hobbyist, the lawn-ornament guy could make any goofy thing he wanted and stick it in his yard. Once he became a pro, he had to give serious thought to his business, his products and ways to expand both. The artisan, on the other hand, received his education in the most rarefied kind of woodworking (at the master's side) and in its dark side (it's tough to make a living building expensive furniture). His formal education didn't prepare him for the truth: Your products and services will be successful only if there is someone willing to buy them. Making that happen is the subject of this chapter.

TURNING YOUR PERSONAL
INTEREST INTO A BUSINESS

In the previous examples, I'm not concluding that you should let others determine what you make. I am a firm believer in what Joseph Campbell calls "following your bliss." What you need to do is find ways to turn your personal interest in woodworking into a profitable business. Most woodworkers do some kinds of work more than others, eventually finding a specialty or developing a reputation for expertise in their chosen field. If you consider how to market your interests now before you start your business, you'll save a lot of painful experimentation later and start seeing profits earlier in the game—without compromising your principles.

The subtitle of this book is *Turning Your Hobby into a Profession*. Your hobby, specialized skill or interest is a great way to get started as a professional woodworker. Hobbyists often have inside knowledge, know their market because they are part of it and are able to spot potential ways to profit from that market. For instance, if you build marquetry jewelry boxes, you know the sources for materials, you know the collector publications, such as newsletters, that might feature these boxes, and you may be a member of an organization that shares an interest in marquetry. When considering a part-time business building these boxes you might ask yourself who buys handmade boxes and how do I reach that audience? The resources and inside knowledge you possess as a hobbyist can get you started in answering those questions. You might find that custom handmade box collecting is one of the hot areas in the collectible market, with galleries doing exhibitions of the work, while arts magazines feature the work of new names in the business. You might discover that it is not only marquetry but the boxes themselves that collectors want, which means that your potential product line can be expanded into other styles and types of boxes. You might even make a crazy science-fiction-style box with a metal flake finish for a gag and have it snapped up by a collector for serious money. And you might find your "crazy" art boxes in demand, keeping you busy on weekends and bringing in a nice second income.

This scenario is totally speculative. Or is it? While I was writing this book I worked with a woodworker who designed and built a line of veneered cigar humidors. His interest came out of his participation in a local cigar club. He connected with a national cigar distributor, and his humidor line is now in its catalog. The catalog company also asked him if he could do similar jewelry boxes because it had customers requesting them as gifts for spouses after the husband dropped several hundred dollars on a humidor. In the process we discovered that there is, in fact, a lot of collector interest in boxes, giving my woodworker friend yet another potential outlet for his work. All from an interest in cigars.

The success or failure of a product line is not an accident. There are steps you can take before you commit to a product or work level. These steps can help you avoid major mistakes and commitments of time and money and find ways to market tough-to-sell services and products such as custom furnishings. They can also help you identify other spin-off items you could market successfully, thus increasing your sales and building your long-term relationship with your customers. The key to success is to plan your product line before you commit to it. This is true whether you are a part-timer crafting wooden bowls or a cabinet shop building dozens of audiovisual centers.

We're going to take a look at how a product line takes form by looking at a fictional woodworking business called Kids and Colors, Inc.

▼ ▼ ▼

A PRODUCT LINE EXAMPLE

Kids and Colors, Inc., didn't start out with a catchy name or a large shop filled with professional tools. It didn't have a bright catalog, and there were no stores featuring its line of brightly colored children's furnishings. It started in a basement with an old table saw and a few power tools. Upstairs from the basement was the home of Joe Tell and his wife and their three young children. The upstairs was important because it was Joe's product-testing lab, and his wife and children were the testers. Joe started out as a hobbyist woodworker building items from plans he bought from magazines. He found it a relaxing diversion from his job as an engineer for the aeronautics industry designing parts that he rarely saw in a finished product. Woodworking also gave him the sense of gratification that comes from building something with his own hands.

Little kids grow up fast and Joe wanted to capture that growth before it became old hat, so he designed a wooden stick that mounted on a doorway and had a sliding measuring block that worked like the ones in doctors' offices. His son would stand under the block, Joe would slide it down and mark his height and the date on a line scored in the wood. Because his son had a thing for dinosaurs, Joe gave the block the shape of a tyrannosaurus head leaning down to bite his son's head. He also finished the stick in bright green, including some dinosaur detailing in other bright colors.

The stick was a hit with everyone who saw it, and Joe started getting requests for sticks from friends and relatives. He thought about selling the plans to a woodworking magazine or making up a bunch and trying to sell them at craft shows in the summer. Before he got a chance to do anything, something serendipitous happened. A friend with one of Joe's sticks showed it to another friend who worked at an educational toy store, and she showed it to her boss who called Joe and asked him how much they sold for.

Since he hadn't sold one yet, Joe said he would have to think about it and promised to call back. Then he did a cost and time estimate, which told him how much it cost to make a stick. When he finished he was surprised to see that each stick cost him about $50, even if he paid himself a small percentage of his income from his day job. Clearly the stick wouldn't work from a price standpoint, and the store manger had told him that wholesale prices (what they paid) were typically half of what the item sold for. That meant the stick would have to sell for around a hundred dollars, a ridiculous sum.

Joe thought about it for a while and figured out how to make 20 sticks on a mini-assembly line. This got him down to $21 dollars each. He called the store manager and asked her what she thought they could sell for. She thought $30 was realistic. He was getting closer. What took the most time and involved the most expense was finishing the stick. Everyone commented on the design and color schemes Joe used, so he couldn't really cut corners there. However, he discovered that he could make a stencil to do the detailing and spray on the paint, saving a lot of time. This further lowered his price to $14 each, and he was in business.

Adding on 20% for profit, he quoted the store buyer a price of $16.80 each and she ordered ten, with the warning that if they went well she'd want more for the Christmas season. She also needed an invoice and a name to bill it to. And did he have any related items?

By the end of that fall Joe had a business called Kids and Colors, Inc. He found a graphic designer who created an eye-catching logo and had tags and instruction sheets printed. He also went to several other kids' shops nearby and took more orders, eventually selling around a hundred sticks and matching dino head coat racks. It was taking quite a bit of his time and he wasn't making any money; in fact, he was out a couple hundred dollars after paying the designer and printer and buying some tools. But he was having a great time, and he knew he was onto something good.

After Christmas, sales dried up, and he and his wife had a discussion about Kids and Colors. They knew they had a potentially profitable business but that they couldn't earn a profit unless they scaled up their production, including adding more products with bigger profit margins. They also had to confront the larger issue of Joe leaving his job and their income taking a plunge. They had some savings, she worked and they weren't big spenders—all good signs for a budding venture—and the aeronautics business was in a period of downsizing and layoffs, meaning Joe's once-secure job was not a sure thing anymore. After a lot of soul searching, they decided to do some research and planning before they burned their bridges.

They started at a bank and quickly learned that they needed a formal business plan, and even then their chances of getting a loan were small. They talked to their friend the store manager and learned that nearly everything she sold was purchased at a large educational-toy trade show in Chicago that took place in June. There they could reach large numbers of buyers, including catalog houses and chain stores, if they wanted. They talked to local craftspeople who sold at arts festivals and learned where the big local shows were and how to contact them. They also went to the library and got several books on business planning and small-business start-ups.

By late spring they had a simple business plan, designs for several pieces of children's furniture, including a foot stool, a toy chest and a coat rack, and they knew how much money they needed to get started. Joe cleaned out the garage to serve as a temporary shop, bought some professional-quality tools, including a high-volume, low-pressure (HVLP) spray setup, and began building several of each piece in different colors and design motifs.

The show in Chicago took place in June, so they had a deadline coming up fast. A photographer friend took photos of the line in her studio in exchange for one of each piece. The prints went to the graphic designer, who put together a one-page full-color sell sheet set up like a catalog page. They had a thousand printed on a heavy glossy stock and attached business cards to every one. They also worked out the pricing of each piece, putting together a wholesale price list on their PC.

The greatest expense they faced was the cost of doing business at the show. Everything about these shows costs money, including travel and accommodations, booth rental, hauling all the materials to the show and paying union scale to have every single item carried in. Before they committed to the show, Joe did some research and found that a lot of small vendors did business out of their hotel rooms and just used the show to schmooze and pass out information. What's more, they could rent a list of attendees and send an invitation, a sell sheet and a letter telling them how to see the line. Joe decided on this approach and limited his mailings to companies in his part of the country. Joe's wife decided two weeks before the show to call everyone on the list, and she did, reaching over half of their prospects. This turned out to be the most effective part of their preparation.

The show weekend was crazy but a lot of fun, especially when they took orders. They worked all weekend, met dozens of other craftspeople and learned a lot about the retail business—more than any book could convey. They also took orders for an alarming number of pieces, particularly Joe's height sticks. It was becoming obvious that working full time and doing the woodworking was going to be tough. The garage was looking pretty small already, and it wouldn't work at all when the winter's cold weather began.

To make a long story shorter, a year later Kids and Colors, Inc., had two employees besides Joe and his wife. They had a shop and office in an old industrial building. While looking at space they met several other wood-workers and ended up farming out the fabrication of some of the parts to a small shop in their building. Joe quit his job in September and things were tight until the Christmas season when their buyers started paying the bills. The next time they hit the trade show they knew people from the year before and were starting to feel like old hands. Several large chain stores ordered their line, convinced by their second appearance at the show that they would be able to deliver. They hadn't equaled Joe's income from the aeronautics job, but they were having a blast and the money was getting better every month.

This is an idealized story. Almost every mistake new business owners typically make was avoided because of the research and planning they did before making a big commitment to the business. They also chose a product line and niche market that was salable, as proven by their first store sales. Few new business owners have the marketing savvy and business sense to create a line, come up with catchy name, hire professional designers to make a good first impression and make the many contacts necessary for success. Yet each of these activities can be done by anyone and will work for any woodworking business, no matter how small.

By starting with a product based on something you are familiar with, testing the waters and developing business skills, you can succeed as a professional woodworker. I'd suggest that as you read through this book you make notes on how you could use each tactic, story or strategy to improve your success. You'll start getting ideas. Jot them in a notebook and decide who would buy them, how much they'd cost to make, etc. Don't forget to take into consideration your interest in the business. A product you hate that makes money can build a business, but being miserable in what you do is not worth it.

Joe could easily have remained a part-time woodworker, built his designs at home in small numbers and sold them locally or at craft shows. He would have done well, much better than most people do with part-time occupations. His decision was to scale up and build a full-time business with growth potential. Either way you choose to do it, you can profit in a woodworking career from the information you'll find in this book.

▼ ▼ ▼

CHAPTER 3

Forms of business

Working with the pros

THE BUSINESS STUFF

As an amateur woodworker, you may already have a shop dedicated to your hobby. It might be a corner of your basement, a garage or perhaps a barn or outbuilding. You've accumulated tools and may also have an inventory of parts, lumber and hardware. Now that you're thinking of becoming a professional, even as a part-timer, you must revise your ideas about how your shop will be set up and run. Some of the things that work well for a casual user will not work well for the pro who, in order to be profitable, must constantly fine-tune his methods.

Changing the way you think about your shop space is only one attribute of starting and running a business. In the next three chapters we're going to look at everything you need to consider when setting up shop as a pro, whether you produce birdhouses or corporate furnishings. Starting a woodworking business involves more than deciding where to put your table saw. You need to get the business part of your shop operating as efficiently as your workspace. By taking care of business planning now, at the beginning, you'll eliminate many potential future problems and headaches.

FORMS OF BUSINESS

Your first decision is to determine what legal form your business will take. Before making this decision, you should consult your attorney and your accountant, since this decision can have a major impact on your tax situation and exposure to any potential liability in the future. While both of these considerations may seem a little scary, they are a normal part of being in business. Taxes, liability, insurance, lawyers and accountants are interrelated, and it will be much easier to deal with them now, at the beginning when things are relatively simple, than later, when a crisis occurs. So don't skip this section if you're serious about going into business.

You have three choices for setting up your business. The simplest, sole proprietorship, is suitable for part-timers working alone and small one-owner shops. Usually, you just file a DBA (Doing Business As) form with your local government and get a tax number from your state tax department. This form registers your company name locally and gives you the necessary paperwork to open a bank account for your business. It does not protect the name from imitators or protect you from personal liability.

JOHN DOE WOODWORKING: SOLE PROPRIETORSHIP

Sole proprietorship means you own 100% of the business, all profits go directly to you and appear as income on your personal tax return, and you are personally liable for any debts or legal claims against your business. If someone sues John Doe Woodworking, John is liable if he is a sole proprietor. There are many advantages to being a sole proprietor. If you work part time as a woodworker and have a salaried job elsewhere, you may be able to write off start-up losses against your regular income at tax time. You are answerable to no one else and can have a piece of the American dream by opening up shop under your own steam. It is the closest we can come to being an explorer or pioneer.

Sole proprietorship is much less complex, from a legal and accounting perspective, than a corporation or partnership. You can dissolve it easily, you do not have to hold legally required meetings and you are not subject to the decisions of others. For many new businesses, it is the way to go, particularly if you will be starting out as a part-timer.

SMITH AND JONES WOODWORKING: PARTNERSHIP

The second option is a partnership. You can only have a partnership with a partner or partners—it is not an option for loners. Partnerships are very controversial among business experts, including your fellow business owners, because almost everyone has a horror story about a partnership gone wrong. They seem to be particularly susceptible to Murphy's Law. The potential problems include division of responsibilities, money, labor, investment and decision making. Partnerships are soluble at any time by any partner unless legally designed otherwise. A falling out with a partner can mean your business is closed, your bank account inaccessible and your customers confused or lost. These pitfalls must be dealt with in your partnership agreement. You must have an agreement, in writing, prepared by an attorney, before entering into any partnership. A word-of-mouth or handshake agreement may legally bind you, but it cannot prepare you for all the possible conflicts that may arise. Some of the books listed in Resources (see p. 150) contain sample partnership agreements that can be used as a basis for your own, should you choose to go this route. By using a basic form and agreeing on details ahead of time, you'll save time and money at your attorney's office.

Partnerships have advantages. A partner shares the load and provides companionship in the often lonely process of business ownership. A great partnership can come about when each partner brings a complementary set of skills to the business. A good people person and an excellent project organizer might make a good team. Complementary woodworking skills or the combination of two existing customer lists can help a new partnership get off the ground successfully. There are economics in sharing tools and tasks that can work in your favor; however, these things can also work against you if both partners are trying to complete similar tasks at the same time. A successful partnership requires constant communication and an ability to plan and work with others.

WOODWORKER, INC.: CORPORATIONS

The third common form of business is the corporation. The corporation has been described as one of the great inventions of mankind. A corporation is an entity of its own. It exists separate from the personal fortunes of its founders and can pass from their hands intact or even outlive them. It pays its own taxes, can be sued and may have many owners in the form of shareholders, which are important considerations. The decision to incorporate is complex and requires expert advice and input from a team of professionals (see pp. 21-24).

The most common reasons for incorporation for very small businesses are protection from liabilities, ownership issues and as a way of raising capital or start-up money. Corporations can provide some protection from personal liability for a business owner. However, protection is by no means guaranteed, particularly if it can be proven that protection from liability was the main reason for incorporation.

For most of us, sole proprietorship is the way to go. If you are setting up a business that will grow into a company with many employees or have a variety of products, you may wish to incorporate. It is much easier to raise money for growth when you have stock to distribute. Incorporation also involves many complex tax issues and angles that are beyond the scope of this book (and change yearly). Again, I recommend seeing a competent accountant and attorney.

Choosing a legal form of business is the first decision you must make when setting up shop. As a part of the decision, you need the services of a group of people that a lot of artist/craftspersons usually try to avoid: Attorneys, accountants and other professional business-service providers. Get your team together now—even if you merely chat on the phone or have an exploratory meeting—and you'll avoid many potential problems later on.

▼▼▼

WORKING WITH THE PROS

You cannot learn and do everything involved in running a business on your own. Simply becoming a proficient woodworker, keeping your shop together, doing quotes and getting work is more than a full-time job. Trying to keep up with tax law, legal considerations, insurance and the myriad issues involved in business ownership would overwhelm even the craziest workaholic. Fortunately you have access to professionals who specialize in knowing these things and helping you understand them. These business professionals should be on your team, however informally, from the beginning.

LAWYERS

Most of us aren't comfortable dealing with lawyers, accountants, insurance brokers and other service providers because their worlds seem so esoteric and incomprehensible to us. It is important to remember that they make their living in exactly the same way a woodworker does: They provide expert advice and skills for a price, a price that will almost always be less than you could do it for yourself. When you shell out $100 an hour for a lawyer, you are gaining access to his or her entire specialized experience and skill base. A lawyer can immediately recognize a problem and tailor a solution that is most beneficial to you, the client. For example, imagine you are considering leasing a commercial space where you can build your woodshop. You look at that space, like it and the owner sends you a lease. When you examine the lease, you find it filled with fine print and statements about "triple net leasing" and a "$5 per square foot plus a common area charge." It discusses fees for snow removal, liability in fires and that natural disasters are the lessee's responsibility and so on. You look at it and, unless you are intimate with the ins and outs of commercial leases, start to panic. Not only that, it lists escalating rents for five years, and the wording makes it seem that you are personally responsible for $40,000 in rent if you sign. Geez! (We'll be looking at some of these terms and realities in the next chapter.)

You start having second thoughts about your whole business. At this point a friend who owns his own business steps in and says, "Go see Paul Smith. He's a lawyer who specializes in small businesses and let him take a look. It'll cost you a few bucks but you'll know exactly what you're getting into and he can renegotiate some of these terms to your advantage."

You meet with Paul, he goes over the lease with you, makes some notes, calls the landlord to clarify some issues and says go ahead and sign, under these conditions. He gives you some advice about your business and recommends an accountant. His advice on the lease saves you hundreds in unnecessary items he got removed and, on top of it all, he recommends you to an associate who wants a cabinet for his stereo system.

While this is an idealized situation, it is not far from reality. A few key things happened: You didn't sign the lease without getting advice, you got a recommendation from a fellow business owner who has dealt with the same problems, and the lawyer you saw specialized in small business. This is vital. A corporate lawyer or a criminal lawyer (to mention just a few specialties) cannot provide the kind of specialized advice you need as a business owner. Get someone who understands the problems you face regularly and your budget.

You also got a referral to an accountant, which can save you time and money. It is not in your attorney's best interest to refer you to an accountant who doesn't fit your needs. Referrals are one of the most important tools of small business. Most of your work and sales, no matter what kind of woodworking you do, will come from referrals. This is the case with almost all small businesses including your professional advisers. Learn to use the referral system and you will benefit in many ways. In my example, your new attorney referred some potential business to you. This happens all the time, particularly as your reputation grows. You'll find referrals discussed throughout this book.

ACCOUNTANTS

Accounting is one of the least understood parts of running a business. Most people think it is bookkeeping, taxes or money. While accounting is all of these things, it is also an information system that can tell you at a glance how your business is doing. Your accountant can show you easy ways to set up your books and bank accounts, make sure you pay your taxes and help you take advantage of the many tax benefits of being self-employed. He can also advise you on the advantages and disadvantages of buying property or large tools, partnerships, selling your business and many other issues concerning money. The statements he prepares can tell you at a glance if you are profitable, how much you are worth, if you have enough money to take on a big job and how you can achieve these things if you are not there yet.

As a small business, you do not necessarily need a certified public accountant (CPA). CPAs go through rigorous training and testing to be qualified to do audits for complex business and tax situations. They charge more because of their expertise. However, a non-CPA may be fine because you are probably not going to require that level of expertise. At the beginning, I don't recommend going to a bookkeeper. Have an accountant help you get started, then use a freelance bookkeeper a few hours a week to maintain the system, if necessary. Most of you running one- or two-person shops can do it yourselves if you have the discipline to keep everything up-to-date all the time. There are many computer software programs to make this easy, and they have the advantage of automatically updating everything every time you make an entry. They can also generate end-of-year and tax statements with a few keystrokes, print out invoices, write checks and keep track of expenses on a job-by-job basis. Most of them use an interface that is very similar to your checkbook and very easy to learn.

If you are realistic and realize that keeping books is not your forte, you should consider getting a part-time bookkeeper after your accountant has helped set up your books. For a few hours per week, these independent business persons can save you hundreds, if not thousands, of dollars in lost time, money and aggravation. Consider them. You can usually find one through a referral from your accountant or ads in local business publications. As you should for all independent contractors, check their references. This small step can save a lot of headaches.

INSURANCE BROKERS

Insurance is a necessary evil in most people's minds. As a self-employed woodworker, you may need several kinds of insurance, including health insurance (you are in a business where serious accidents can happen), insurance to cover your loss of income in the event of an accident or illness, property insurance for your shop so that you are not wiped out by a fire or disaster, and liability insurance in case someone is injured or hurt by your actions. Having to arrange for all of these types of insurance can be overwhelming. You may have the good fortune to be covered by a spouse's health policy or you may be able to maintain one from a current or previous job, if you are part time. Otherwise, you can probably find a plan administered for small businesses or perhaps by an artist/craftsperson group. Ask your fellow small business owners, the Chamber of Commerce or your local business development office.

For property and liability you need an agent who specializes in business insurance, particularly small-business insurance. There are policies tailored to every kind of situation, and you should shop around for both price and an agent who understands your needs or will take the time to learn them. Insurance is complex, and a detailed discussion of it is beyond the scope of this book. However, I would like to pass on a few thoughts. When you insure your shop and vehicle against loss, get full replacement value. That great old table saw may not do well in an insurance claim unless you can show how much it would cost you to replace it. Keep a detailed inventory of all your tools and any significant supplies you keep on hand, and keep it in some location other than your shop. A video inventory with a soundtrack of you reading serial numbers and relevant specs may help in a major fire or loss. This inventory will be important to your accountant because of amortization, a process that allows you to depreciate equipment over several years.

One of the best ways to keep property insurance costs down is to have a high deductible, say $1,000 or more. Over time, the savings in premiums will far outweigh the occasional small loss from theft or oversight. This is also valuable for vehicle insurance. Increasing your deductible on your health insurance to $5,000 will sharply reduce your payments, but you will be responsible for all noncatastrophic bills. This strategy protects you from losing everything if you sustain a major injury or contract a long-term illness. It is a worst-case scenario but much better than being uninsured.

Liability insurance can be hard to afford, yet it is important for a number of reasons. Many commercial and savvy individual customers will require proof that you have liability insurance before they will contract work from you. They want to know that they are protected if something you do causes damage on their premises. I have heard stories of fires caused by open containers of wood finish left on jobs, injuries caused by poor construction or installations, poisoning of infants by toxic finishes and a host of other horrors. In every case like these you could be liable for damages. In your shop, accidents involving employees or customers are a possibility. Get your liability insurance and make sure you tell potential clients you are insured. It may get your bid moved to the top of the pile over a competitor who was not forthcoming about insurance. This is just one example of the many ways you can use necessary evils such as insurance as marketing tools.

As a small-business owner you'll be coping with all of these things and more, which can be overwhelming. Just remember that by taking things one step at a time and using professionals to help you, you will be fine. As you do business you'll be working with many other business pros, including designers, real estate agents and others who serve small businesses. Further on in the book we'll look at how to utilize these other valuable resources to help your woodworking business prosper.

SETTING UP SHOP

The word *shop* is music to a woodworker's ears, especially the hobbyist who may have had to live with a limited amount of space or less-than-adequate tools. One of the most alluring aspects of going pro is the opportunity to build your dream shop. After all, now that you are a professional, you can justify spending money on a professional workspace, right? Even better, you can get some of those cool gizmos you've been ogling in catalogs and magazines. Well, maybe we're jumping the gun. It's time to back up and take a good look at the differences between a hobbyist woodshop and a professional operation dedicated to efficiency and profit.

Your home shop will probably be the same as your pro shop when you start out, particularly if you are going to try woodworking part time. Eventually, you may want to rent a commercial space or build an addition or outbuilding dedicated to your home business. Because constructing these more commercial shops is a complex issue and represents an opportunity that may come only once in your business life, we'll take a detailed look at upgrading your shop in the next chapter. For now I'll discuss your present shop or the one you're setting up. This shop may be in a corner of a basement or garage, in a den or perhaps in a shed in the yard.

If you're like many casual woodworkers, your shop is a mishmash of odd tools, hardware, wood bits and pieces and a work table or two. It is organized by chance and works fine as an occasional workspace. However, now that you're going to start selling your work, you'll be spending a lot more time in your shop and you'll need to set it up to be efficient and comfortable. At the beginning, when you may not be busy, you can consider how to rearrange your shop and plan your tool purchases and inventory-handling needs.

Planning a professional shop has similar requirements, whether you are rearranging a home shop or laying out 2,000 sq. ft. of commercial space. Even the individual who carves decoys, for instance, has a variety of processes he goes through for each completed bird carving. He starts with raw, roughsawn wood and ends up with a hand-carved and painted decoy worth hundreds or thousands of dollars. Each piece goes through similar steps, from initial concept to completion. Whether you build cabinets, carve carousel horses or fabricate marquetry music boxes, you have a process that works best for each piece. The first step in planning your shop is to look at that process and create a timeline that includes each manufacturing step and lists the tools, space and materials it requires. Writing down and organizing your procedures will tell you a great deal about how to work more efficiently and be cost effective by eliminating bottlenecks and repetition.

Your written process plan will be usable for many of the concepts covered in this book. A process plan is an excellent aid to pricing, for instance, allowing you to break down labor, time and materials for each step of construction. This can be a great help when you need to price a new piece or determine whether your prices are profitable and competitive. We don't get efficient to *save* money; we get efficient to *make* money. Professionals are always looking for better ways to do things, and this simple exercise can help you think about your work in a more professional (and profitable) manner.

▼▼▼

A PROCESS PLAN

Raymond Chase, a fictional character, is a well-known professional decoy carver from West Virginia. His decoys are prized by collectors for their detail, accuracy and lifelike poses. After carving as a hobby for several years, Ray began to get requests for birds and eventually reached the point where his decoys sold for thousands of dollars and customers had to wait for up to a year to purchase one. He still works out of his home in the hills of rural West Virginia.

Because Chase's decoys are scientifically accurate, planning is vital to each carving. Ray is represented by a gallery that specializes in decoys and other natural carvings, and he determines what birds he will carve. If he were less well known or just getting started, he might want to take commissions from customers for specific birds or poses. If that was the case, the first step would be meeting with the customer (in person, by phone or through the mail) to determine the type of project, set a price and devise a schedule for completing the work. Since Ray's birds are always in demand, his gallery handles the sales, and he simply does the carving. Here is the process Ray Chase uses to plan, carve and finish one of his famous decoys (see the flow chart on p. 28).

The first step for Ray is to choose the species of bird to carve along with an appropriate pose. To help get ideas, he'll usually spend time searching through his library of bird books and photos taken in the field. Whenever possible, he tries to see the live bird to help capture its feeling and coloring. Once he's decided, he makes detailed life-size drawings and watercolors of various angles and poses of the bird. These drawings will determine the final look of the decoy.

With drawings in hand, Ray heads for the shop. He starts by cutting a carving blank from a large piece of basswood. If the decoy is larger than the basswood he has on hand, he'll plane, joint, and glue-up a number of smaller pieces to form a blank.

To carve the decoy, Ray begins by transferring the drawings to his blank. He then roughs out the shape on the band saw. Next, with a steady hand and an electric carver, Ray carves the shape of the bird in about two hours. At this point, he switches to a set of chip-carving knives to finish carving and add the final details. By constantly referring to the photos and drawings he's made, Ray can complete the decoy in around eight hours.

All that's left is to add a finish. Ray starts with two coats of primer, followed by several basic colors applied with an airbrush. The fine details are painted on with artist's brushes. To protect the decoy, a final coat of matte lacquer is sprayed on. Before Ray packs up the decoy for shipment to a gallery and invoices it, he takes a photo of it for his portfolio.

These steps are enlightening in a number of ways. A comprehensive tool list can be compiled. There are definite work stations that are used for different tasks. Material purchasing and handling must be considered. Research, photography and billing are included as vital parts of the process. The hours are based on a minimum of one hour for each task because of setup, but in some cases, prep work is done for several projects all at once. Ray's total hours are 34.5. He adds on 5.5 hours for profit, totaling 40. His materials are inexpensive in quantity, but his original inventory of paint and wood was fairly expensive. If his bird sells for $2,500, of which Ray receives $1,500 after a gallery commission of 40% (yes, 40%!), he is averaging $37.50 per hour before expenses and overhead. This figure reflects the fact that Ray is highly skilled and has spent years building a reputation as one of the country's preeminent bird carvers.

PROCESS PLAN FLOW CHART FOR A SPECIALIZED WOODCARVING SHOP

There are big differences in the way a pro woodworker and an amateur woodworker will do certain tasks. The hobbyist probably buys wood in small quantities and may get it pre-milled. The pro will have trucks delivering large amounts of rough lumber that must be stored, moved into the shop, planed and shaped, etc. Each of these labor-intensive operations can be made much easier by planning work flow by visualizing the steps taken to execute a typical project. The chart at right shows the steps discussed on the previous page for Ray Chase's decoy-making business.

Step 1
Research bird for decoy
Location: Library/office
Tools: Books
Materials: Notebook
Time: 4 hours

▼

Step 2
Drawings for decoy
Location: Library/office
Tools: Drafting table
Materials: Paper, watercolors
Time: 4 hours

▼

Step 3
Prepare carving blanks
Location: Shop/large tool area
Tools: Planer, jointer, table saw, clamps
Materials: Basswood, glue
Time: 4 hours (makes six blanks)

▼

Step 4
Transfer drawings to blank
Location: Shop bench
Tools: Pencil
Materials: None
Time: 1.5 hours

▼

Step 5
Rough out shape
Location: Shop
Tools: Band saw
Materials: None
Time: 2 hours

▼

Step 6
Hand carve bird
Location: Shop bench
Tools: Electric carver, chip-carving knives
Materials: None
Time: 8 hours

▼

Step 7
Prime bird for finish
Location: Shop finishing area
Tools: HVLP sprayer
Materials: Oil-based primer
Time: 1 hour

Step 8
Spray basic colors
Location: Shop finishing area
Tools: Airbrush
Materials: Artist's colors
Time: 2 hours

▼

Step 9
Fine-detail painting
Location: Shop finishing area
Tools: Artist's brushes
Materials: Artist's colors
Time: 4 hours

▼

Step 10
Clear lacquer overcoat
Location: Shop finishing area
Tools: HVLP sprayer
Materials: Lacquer
Time: 1 hour

▼

Step 11
Photograph for portfolio
Location: Copystand
Tools: Camera, lights
Materials: Film
Time: 1 hour

▼

Step 12
Pack and ship
Location: Shipping table
Tools: Packing tape dispenser
Materials: Tape, box, label, postage
Time: 1 hour

▼

Step 13
Prepare invoice
Location: Library/office
Tools: Computer, software, printer
Materials: Stationery, postage
Time: 1 hour

A SHOP PLAN

If you have broken down the assembling of your typical project into steps, as we did with Ray's, then you already have an idea of what your shop should look like. Let's take a look at Ray's workplaces. One of Ray's most important work areas is nowhere near his woodshop. Ray's library/den contains his desk with computer, bookcases full of reference books, a comfortable chair with good lighting for reading and a drawing table facing a north window. A flat file cabinet contains his drawings and paintings of birds. This room serves a number of the steps in his process plan. Research, business matters, drawing and planning and the occasional meeting with his gallery rep take place here. It is clean and conspicuously free of sawdust and paint smells.

Before we step into Ray's shop, we take a walk through a garage filled with racks of rough wood. Here, Ray stores quantities of the materials he uses regularly and he keeps track of dryness and quality. The garage is accessible to the large trucks that deliver his stock, and he can easily load directly into his racks from the truck, an important consideration for the solo woodworker.

The extra-wide back door of Ray's garage leads into his shop. Here we can see the logic of its layout. A table next to the planer receives the rough lumber. After several passes through the planer, the wood travels along the wall to the jointer and finally reaches the table saw for trimming. A workbench backed with a large number of clamps on a rack is the station where the wood is glued and clamped into large pieces. From here we reach the band saw, which is out in the center of the room to make it easy to maneuver wood around the blade. From there the blocks get stacked in a dry corner. On the other side of the room is a carving station with a European-style bench and a comfortable chair for detail work. Lighting is directly overhead, and a gooseneck detail light is close at hand.

Ray does his spraying in a booth that once served as a mud room. It has an explosion-proof exhaust fan, a compressor and fireproof storage for solvents and lacquer. An adjustable table-mounted clamp holds the decoy via a screw in the bottom.

Detail painting takes place back in the shop on a table next to the carving table. Ray has a portable lighting setup to photograph his work. By using the same setup all the time, he rarely has to adjust lighting or exposure levels. A professional photographer friend helped him set it up, and it is less expensive and time consuming than having a pro shoot his work.

Finally Ray has a small table to pack his work. He has packing materials, boxes, tape and shipping labels. A small postal scale completes the setup.

This ideal shop works directly out of Ray's process plan. Materials are easily handled. Operations requiring large power tools and generating large amounts of dust are grouped together to take advantage of a central dust collector attached to the tools. The tools are placed in a work-flow order that makes it easy for one person to handle each step. When the pieces are reduced to carving size they move to other areas scaled to detail work, including carving, painting, photographing and shipping. All of the business activities, such as billing and sales, take place in a clean dust-free environment that keeps Ray's computer working well.

Ray Chase is a successful woodworker who turned a specialized hobby into a profession. One of his secrets of success is his desire to seek a better, more efficient way to work. When you look at the relationship between Ray's work methods and his shop layout, you can see this attitude in action. Whether you work out of a corner of your basement or are looking at commercial shop space, spending time analyzing your needs can mean big savings in money, time and aggravation. The work-flow chart on the facing page outlines the points at which you can study and improve your business.

The process plan does more than help with shop layout. It tells you what tools are most important and helps determine when and whether you need to change your shop to better serve your purposes as a professional. In the next chapter we'll look at home vs. commercial space and amateur vs. professional tools for the shop. By making these plans now and basing your purchasing and leasing decisions on them, you'll save plenty of money and be more profitable in your new profession.

WORK-FLOW CHART FOR A SMALL WOODSHOP

This chart shows typical steps in a custom shop. Each represents a point where the shop owner can improve or learn more for future use. Knowing the time, money (materials and overhead) and labor involved at each step can help with future estimates or product development, shop planning and tool purchases.

Marketing
Make initial contact with customer; complete sale and estimate; sign contract or purchase order. For some this step may include booking gallery shows or festival appearances.

▼

Design or product development
Research; make drawings; price materials and components; get design approval from customer.

▼

Ordering, planning & budgeting
Order materials; plan work required; get cost estimates; take delivery of materials; store materials.

▼

Dimensioning lumber, cut lists & diagrams
Pick through lumber; plane and joint to dimensions; plan and execute cuts, etc.

▼

Final preparation
Prep for fabrication: cut, sand, join, turn, etc. for final assembly.

▼

Assembly
Complete joinery; assemble.

▼

Finishing
Sand; paint, stain or dye; finish.

Add outsourced components
Add hardware and any other elements not made in shop.

▼

Ship and/or install
Pack; ship or deliver; install if necessary.

▼

Follow-up
Check with customer for satisfaction.

▼

Billing
Send final invoice or bill; do bookkeeping; check profit and loss on job for future comparison.

▼

Marketing follow-up
Send thank-you note; request referrals; add to current customer list for future contact.

▼

Future planning & evaluation
Determine what you did right and wrong, how you could improve work and profits and how you may sell this project again.

FINDING THE RIGHT SPACE

The space you work in has an impact on the success of your business and the enjoyment you get from that business. By considering the processes you use while creating your products and dealing with your customers before you plan your workspace, you'll ensure that the space functions efficiently.

What defines a shop that "works"? Efficiency, comfort, accessibility, expandability and safety are prime considerations. You must store supplies and finished work, have clean areas for office work and finishing, and arrange your tools to keep things flowing without having to rearrange and set them up constantly. Depending on the kind of work you do, you may have to meet customers at your shop for planning and sales, possibly requiring a display area or retail or gallery space. If this is the case, cleanliness and safety take on added importance, from both the customer's point of view and a legal one.

Zoning, liability, safety, parking, access and other issues become more than convenience when you are running a business. They become legal requirements, particularly if you live in a relatively populated area and have customers visit your shop regularly. You must also cope with electrical, dust collection, plumbing and other systems that can be both expensive and complex.

HOME SHOPS vs. COMMERCIAL SPACE

In this chapter we'll look at how to set up a commercial woodworking shop. Whether you work at home or in a commercial space you rent or own is probably your first decision when planning your shop. Home shops are fine for getting started, particularly if you make smaller pieces and work part time. However, many woodworkers soon find that the dust, accessibility and noise of a shop can overflow into their home life, often conflicting with their family's comfort level. When you're working as a professional woodworker it can be nice to get out of the shop at the end of a long day and go home to a clean, quiet, dust-free environment.

The home shop is also limited when it comes to processes such as material handling and finishing. Moving quantities of wood up and down basement steps and through narrow doorways quickly become tiresome. A primary difference between hobbyist woodworkers and the pros is the use of dimensioned lumber. As a professional you'll soon discover that paying a premium for milled lumber is not cost effective, particularly when you need quantities and unusual dimensions. You may eventually be purchasing sawmill rough-cut lumber and doing your own planing and dimensioning. This can require dry storage and room to maneuver. In addition to noise, you also create remarkable amounts of chips and sawdust, which may require commercial trash removal.

A home shop works well for small projects that don't require large materials and tools. Woodcarvers or boxmakers might get by with a basement shop and a garage or outbuilding where they can store wood and do milling and larger cuts. Likewise, if you are doing one or two pieces of furniture a month, you can get by with a small shop. Even then, you'll find yourself constantly cleaning, rearranging and moving things around to prepare for finishing and delivery. Eventually most woodworkers start dreaming of that perfect shop away from the basement or garage.

The decision to move out of your home shop is a significant one in many ways. It represents a major commitment to woodworking as a profession, both psychologically and financially. This is a very good reason to move your business out of the house. Unlike the home offices we hear about regularly, woodworking is a manufacturing process and often works best in its own environment. The psychological benefits are just as important. Out of the house, faced with overhead and a space devoted to work, you are forced to focus on your woodworking as a profession rather than a hobby. Everything changes, from the suppliers you deal with to the prices your work commands in the marketplace. You are taken more seriously by your potential customers. Your time is dedicated to work without the alluring distractions of being at home.

I have found that getting into a professional, work-oriented space is vital to the long-term success of any small business. Even home businesses suffer when the space they occupy is shared with household activities and interruptions. I highly recommend that you seriously consider moving your business away from your house as soon as it is practical, even if it means a move into a building on your property. You'll feel and act differently, get more work done and the work you do will be more profitable.

▼ ▼ ▼

PLANNING THE MOVE

Before you take the plunge and rent or purchase shop space, it's imperative that you do some serious planning. Leasing a space can be expensive and involves many details you may not have considered. The planning you do before you start looking at space can save you money and help you avoid many problems in the future. It also helps you make decisions about the size of your business, the money you'll need to bring in and the kinds of work you do and will do in the future. This kind of planning is no different from what you do when you design a new piece of furniture or learn how to master a new joinery technique. It involves some research and requires you to visualize where you're going and how you'll get there.

Visualization is a simple technique that helps with many of the decisions involved in choosing and planning a new workspace. It also helps you determine whether the space you're considering is something you really want. You simply imagine yourself, in the not-too-distant future, in your perfect shop space. Construct the space in your mind, giving it all the necessary details. Think about the lighting, the layout, the entrances and the office space attached. Put yourself in the space and look around, adjusting things until you feel comfortable. It is important when visualizing your space to include sounds, climate, even the smell of sawdust or air coming in a window.

Because this is an imaginary space, you have complete flexibility in your choices. You can put any tools you need in the shop and give yourself a nice design area with a computer and a comfortable place to make coffee or meet with customers. This exercise helps you to understand what kinds of things are important for you to have in your workspace. While your shop may not actually have all the amenities you can imagine, you can identify those things that will make a basic difference and ensure that your new space includes them.

Fortunately, this exercise is an easy one for most woodworkers. Everyone fantasizes about an ideal shop, the tools it contains, the feeling of being surrounded by wood and what it would be like to open the doors each morning. Creating a shop in your mind can help you recognize the space you need when you are out looking for it.

WORKSPACE CHECKLIST

After you visualize your workspace, start a checklist of what you want and need. Following are some items to consider. Since every woodworker has some specialized requirements, you'll be adding more of your own to the list, while others may not be relevant to your needs.

Location

We've all heard the cliché about location being the three most important qualities of any real estate decision, and for most uses this is correct. Location is the primary factor determining price or rent, which is a major consideration. However, for a woodworker location is much less important because the priorities are different. In fact, your ideal location is probably a terrible location for most other businesses.

You should consider most of the items on the list as criteria when choosing a location. Size, accessibility, zoning and many other things are important. If you will be meeting customers and clients at your shop, then you should consider your location from a marketing point of view. Is it hard to find? Will you have to spend advertising dollars just to get your prospects to your door? Or will they come to you wherever you are? Your marketing plan and market will help answer these questions (see Chapter 9).

Rent or purchase price

Space is either leased or purchased. In a purchase you should use a qualified real estate agent who specializes in commercial real estate and represents your interests (a "buyer's" agent). Such a person will provide expert knowledge about the ins and outs of your area's real estate market, including pricing and help with many of the questions on the workspace checklist. You also need an attorney with commercial real estate experience who represents your interests only, and I emphasize *only* your interests. Don't rely on the seller's or the bank's attorney, since he or she is not committed to watch out for your interests. Only a lawyer paid by you will effectively represent your interests.

Even when leasing, a real estate agent can be a great help. The agent knows the market, the rates and many of the options that must be considered. Working in conjunction with your attorney, the agent can negotiate on your behalf, saving you money and avoiding potential pitfalls.

Price is generally determined by a number of factors, such as square footage, location, usage, who pays what and other variables. Be sure to find out who pays for what and what is or is not included. When renting, commercial lease rates are usually quoted as price-per-square-foot-per-year rather than a monthly fee. This can be confusing until you get a handle on how it works. In my area you can rent commercial manufacturing space for around $3.50 per sq. ft., including heat. If you rent a 1,000-sq.-ft. shop

(20 ft. by 50 ft.) you would pay $3,500 per year, or $292 per month. If you are in a building with other tenants you may have to pay a common area fee of an additional number of square feet per year, perhaps (in our example) 100 sq. ft. This adds about $35 per month to your expense. Add in waste removal, cleaning fees, parking fees, utilities and any other variables and you have your rent figure. Read your lease before you sign and make sure you understand what you pay extra for and what is included.

Up-front cash required

When planning a move it is very important to know how much cash you must invest in up-front fees. These include security deposits (often two to three months rent), utility deposits (remember, like everything, these are negotiable), insurance costs (proof of insurance may be required by the landlord or bank), attorney's fees, remodeling costs (may be shared or paid by landlord, be sure to ask) and other fees required by your local and state governments. This amount can be considerable, and the negotiating you do at the beginning can mean lowering your initial investment, so question every up-front deposit and ask for relief wherever possible.

Square footage

In the last chapter I recommended you do a process plan to determine the most efficient way to set up your shop. This plan can also be a great help in deciding how much space you need. The size of your tools, the space required for maneuvering around them, storage, finishing, office and display areas, shipping and receiving, bathrooms and common areas must be considered. If you can, err slightly on the plus side when picking an ideal number.

In the real world, you will seldom find an ideal space for rent. Odd-size buildings or spaces may mean that some of the footage you pay for is not as useful as you'd like. Try to negotiate a lower rate for wasted space if possible. Keep in mind that you may want more space in the future without incurring the major expense and work of a move. It might be cheaper in the long run to take a larger space now.

Dimensions and layout

When you find a potential space, try adapting your process plan to see if it will work in the new space. An odd-shaped room may not affect one kind of woodworking process, while another may be unable to function there. Plan now to ensure that the space you are considering will fit your needs.

Access

Access is very important for woodworkers. You will need access to a loading dock for deliveries and shipments; a freight elevator, if you are on an upper floor; a pallet jack, if you receive shipments on pallets; and wide doorways and hallways for maneuvering. See if there is another business in the building from which you can borrow a pallet jack or forklift for occasional use, or plan on buying one (another up-front expense). Make sure you have access to bathrooms, water lines and electrical circuit breakers. If customers come to your shop, there must be clear and safe access. If you regularly deal with the public you may be required to provide access for individuals with physical disabilities.

Utilities

Utilities are heat, ventilation and air conditioning, a.k.a. HVAC; communications lines, such as telephone, cable and ISDN lines; electricity; water; plumbing and waste removal (sewage). Make sure all are available (especially in rural areas) and that they can handle your requirements. This may mean access to three-phase electric lines in particular, since many professional tools require this kind of power source. You can't work without heat, water and airflow, particularly if you need to install dust-collection systems. Find out who pays for what, what deposits are required and who can make changes and installations. In many commercial buildings you cannot do utility work yourself and must use licensed contractors approved by the local zoning board. You may also be required to use union labor in certain areas. Ask in advance.

Overestimate your utility requirements, and on a yearly basis be sure to consider the expenses involved. A space with landlord-provided heat may be much cheaper in the long run than one you heat yourself. Ask about the expenses incurred by previous or similar tenants when talking to the local utilities. They may be able to provide an estimated utility bill based on prior or similar usage.

Airflow, windows and lighting

These items not only contribute to your comfort, they may be significant from a health and safety perspective. Can you open the windows? Is there access to air-handling systems? Will natural light provide a significant savings over artificial? You'll be spending a lot of time here; on a gut level, is it comfortable? Can you keep it clean and have dust-free areas for finishing and display or office work? Many commercial buildings are very dusty. Do your neighbors generate chemical odors and fumes? Can you vent finishing fumes without disturbing neighbors?

Ceiling height

One big advantage of many commercial spaces is high ceilings. A 12-ft. ceiling can give you maneuvering room, extra storage space, room for dust collection and lighting systems and the ability to fabricate tall pieces. The only disadvantage is extra height must also be heated and/or cooled.

Room for office and/or display areas

For many reasons your office space must be physically separate from your shop floor. Noise, dust and distractions are eliminated when you can use an alcove or build a room that can be sealed off from the shop. This also helps to keep the office functions separate from the shop functions, allowing you to change hats and focus on the task at hand without distraction.

If your customers will be coming to you, you'll need an area to meet them and go over your work and/or a display area or gallery space. If your customers rarely come to your shop, you may be able to combine a design or drafting area with a meeting room. Galleries and stores require retail-type space that you will probably want to keep separate from the noisy proximity of a shop. Location is a primary consideration when picking a retail or walk-in space for marketing your work. Low-traffic locations require large amounts of advertising to pull in customers, while high-traffic locations have high rents. You can weigh one over the other, but unless you plan on becoming an advertising expert or hiring one, I recommend spending the rent money on a high-traffic location for retail use.

Zoning

It's important to check on the zoning designation of the space you are considering and what usage that designation allows and disallows. This is extremely critical and must be spelled out in the lease. Noise, dust and vehicle restrictions can hobble your business. Parking requirements, access requirements and permits can cost you big bucks. Learn what you can or cannot do in and around your space. Don't depend on a promise of getting an exception or rule change from the zoning board unless your lease is subject to your receiving such a change. Consult your real estate agent and lawyer. Call your town or city about required permits and ask neighboring business owners about their experiences.

Amount of remodeling required

Cheap space is often raw, unimproved space and making improvements can be costly. However, this space is also difficult to rent so many landlords will make improvements as part of a rental agreement. If they offer to make changes prior to your taking possession, take them up on the offer before you sign and write it in, including a schedule with completion dates. Once you've signed and moved in you will find it hard to get action on verbal agreements so take care of it beforehand in writing. Once again, plumbing, waste, electrical and communication lines are vital. Get them run into your space before you sign or negotiate an allowance for the work.

Remodeling is subject to zoning and building-permit rules and may cost you more than you think. Try to complete all of your major remodeling before you move in. It's a lot easier to get it done before you fill the space with tools and wood.

Safety and cleanup

Dust collection and health and safety issues are major concerns of commercial woodworkers. Plan your safety and environmental systems before you move in and you'll avoid many legal and construction problems. Dust collection is a fact of life, along with proper storage of chemicals and other potentially hazardous materials. You'll be subject to inspections for fire and occupational safety, and your insurance company will also have requirements. Take care of these safety considerations at the beginning, and you'll live longer and enjoy your work more while being in compliance.

Trash collection and disposal

If you've been working at home, trash removal is probably something you take for granted. In a commercial space, it is usually your responsibility to get rid of trash, and it can represent a significant outlay in money and time. Woodworking generates a lot of scraps and sawdust. You may need to rent a dumpster service, find a user for sawdust (my brother sends hardwood sawdust to the local mounted police station for horse bedding) or arrange to sell or give away your scrap. It can be burned, used for school projects, ground up for wood products or dumped in a legal dump.

Ventilation and fire protection

Local law may require sprinkler systems, ventilation, and access and egress via fireproof stairs and fire escapes. Make sure you're not liable for installing these expensive permanent building additions. A friend of mine who renovated an old building for use as a restaurant found out two days before opening that a $20,000 sprinkler system was required by law. She never recovered from the unexpected last-minute expense and went out of business a year later, leaving her landlord with a nice new sprinkler system (and restaurant). You'll also need an approved fire extinguisher in good condition with a contract for regular inspection and recharging.

Noise consideration for you and your neighbors

Woodworking is inherently noisy. Be sure that the noise you make does not bother your neighbors, including those above or below you. You can install soundproofing materials but it can get expensive and requires planning by an expert. Always use noise-reducing ear protectors when you're working in the shop. Hearing loss is no joke, and constant exposure to high-decibel noise is exhausting and dangerous.

Storage space

Is there additional storage space on the premises that can be included at a lower rate or for free with the lease or purchase? Often you can negotiate for the use of unmarketable space to use as storage. This can free up your valuable shop space while allowing you to keep your materials nearby. You would be able to save money by purchasing materials in larger quantities, or you could take advantage of sales or seasonable availability. You can also avoid the expense of heating space filled with wood or supplies that don't require a controlled environment.

Parking

How many parking spots do you get with your lease or purchase? Do you have all-day access to a loading dock? Can large trucks get into your lot or alley? Do you have a lot? Does the zoning require a certain amount of parking? Do you need to designate disabled parking spaces? Who pays? Finding answers to these questions is absolutely vital.

Ambiance

The building I share with a number of woodshops and artists has some very inexpensive space for lease in the basement. It is dry and warm and dark and creepy. No one I know wants to work down there for any other reason than the fact that it is cheap. But is it? If you are miserable and cannot wait to get out of your shop each day, you will not succeed in your business. The ambiance of your place is very important. A pleasant and functional workspace can mean the difference between enjoying what you're doing or merely enduring it.

Expandability

When you are considering a move into a new, expanded workplace it can be difficult to imagine needing more space. Yet, in planning a business, it is vital to consider your long-term needs and possibilities. If you have any inkling that you may require more space in the future, look for space that is easily expandable and try to negotiate that expansion into your lease in the form of a "Right of First Refusal" on adjacent space. This gives you first shot at an adjacent space if it becomes available. Expanding outward from an existing space can be easier and cheaper than moving somewhere else, and you don't have to pull out this list and start over from the beginning. The cost of moving is exchanged for the lower cost of remodeling.

You can consider moving just the office, design or finishing functions to a nearby space if contiguous space is not available. This may even have the advantage of cutting down on noise, dust or chemical contamination between sensitive areas.

There is another side of the expansion consideration: Perhaps you wish to downsize, eliminating space, changing focus or subbing out some work to others. All the factors we've considered can help you make such a decision.

Planning and finding a new shop are exciting and frustrating. In spite of the apparent problems I've listed, it is really not that hard to find good space for your woodworking business. Almost every town and city has many old manufacturing buildings that are no longer practical for large companies but are ideal for small businesses such as yours. Enterprising landlords have learned that they can divide these buildings into lofts and offer flexible space to craftspeople like you. There are also many small freestanding buildings that make great shops. You can have fun as you scout out buildings and make inquiries. Often the shop you are looking for is tucked behind another building or lying empty next to a railroad track, ready to be rented cheap and adapted to your needs. If you are creative, you'll find that ideal space.

Consider sharing a space or looking at buildings that house other woodworking businesses. Artists' studios are also good so long as noise is not a problem.

Once you've found a space, you'll need to consider the tools and work-space you'll need. Professional tools are a major difference between the hobbyist woodworker and the pro.

▼▼▼

TOOLS FOR WOODWORKING

In-depth discussions of the merits of one tool vs. another are beyond the scope of this book; however, the decision-making process you go through as a pro when you buy and use tools is markedly different from that of an amateur. Professionals must make their tool purchases based on business considerations rather than personal desires. You will be making a major investment in both woodworking tools and business tools, and the decisions you make now can determine how profitable you are in the future.

The tools in your shop serve one main purpose: They make you more efficient. They save time, material and money and help eliminate mistakes if used properly. Professional-quality tools are held to standards different from the lightweight tools you manage with as a hobbyist. They often run for many hours every day, they must always maintain a high level of accuracy, they must handle heavy loads with ease, and parts and accessories must be sturdy and readily available. To achieve these things, the tools will be heavy, require large, steady power sources, require regular maintenance and be easy to use and set up. These tools cost more but save many headaches. In the long run, you simply cannot get by with inferior tools. A breakdown or inaccurate series of cuts can mean the loss of days of work and ruined materials. To put it simply, buy the best you can afford.

The decision to purchase a tool should be based on your product line, the services you provide and the type of work you do. You should be able to see an immediate and regular savings in time and money. Your accountant (see Chapter 3) will depreciate your tools over several years, resulting in a gradual tax savings. Large tools can be leased with monthly payments. The decision to purchase or lease is simply a business decision: Will the tool earn more and save more than the monthly lease payment? Is it likely to become obsolete during the next few years? Or will your needs be changing over time? The answers to these questions will help you make purchase and leasing decisions.

Used power tools can be a good deal, particularly with large, simple tools such as table saws. Many time-tested designs have been around for years, and upgrade and repair kits are available for most brand names. Check out auctions and going-out-of-business sales with a specific shopping list, and avoid impulse purchases.

Keep an up-to-date inventory of all your tools, including purchase prices, dates, serial numbers and warranty information. Keep a copy at home in case of fire or theft, and you'll be able to get up and running much faster. This inventory will mean significant savings at tax time, and your accountant should have a current copy.

Your process plan and the products and services you offer will ultimately determine your tool purchases. In turn, the tools you own and plan to purchase have a direct impact on the shop space and utility requirements we discussed earlier in this chapter. Even if you can't afford a certain tool or upgrade in the beginning, you should plan on getting it and include it in your shop plans. When you can afford the purchase, you'll be ready to put the tool into action right away without requiring more space or a re-arrangement of your shop. I firmly believe that you should plan your ideal setup at the start because people have a tendency to work toward goals they have spelled out in advance. Planning for future purchases often accelerates your ability and desire to make them.

▼▼▼

TOOLS FOR BUSINESS

The other kind of tools you'll need are business tools, such as office furniture and what I like to call communications tools. These include fax machines and modems, computers, printers and software, telephones and answering machines or voice mail and access to on-line services and the Internet. These are no longer gimmicks or luxury items. They are the tools that help you to compete with larger businesses anywhere in the world. You must be accessible in every way possible. Soon many of these pipelines in and out of your shop will converge, but until then you need all of them. A good-quality fax machine is absolutely essential. You'll use it to send and receive bids, specifications, order products and materials, invoice customers and communicate over long distance.

Cordless phones have made it easy to stay in touch while you're working. Always take calls in person whenever possible. If you can't take a call, make sure your answering machine or voice mail is clear, can take a lengthy message and that you respond quickly. Sign up for an on-line service like America Online, Compuserve or one of the many Internet providers. For a small monthly fee you'll get an e-mail address, access to the Internet's World Wide Web, which is the business forum of the computer nets, and you'll be able to communicate quickly all over the country and the world for almost nothing. I regularly exchange e-mail with a woodworking client in Malaysia, and my total cost is around $3 an hour. It beats faxes, phones and regular mail.

Computers are becoming a fixture at work and at home. Perhaps the biggest change in the computer world is the new understanding that computers excel as communications devices. Besides e-mail, you can compose and send letters, bids, invoices, drawings, do your books, order materials and keep inventory without having to know anything about programming. Software of every kind is available and easy to use no matter what brand of machine you buy. The Internet allows you access to suppliers, research, woodworking discussion groups and Web sites and does not care where you are or what you do. Your clients are getting used to this new world at the same rate as you are and becoming more open to dealing with small shops regardless of location. Your computer and other business tools make it possible to "act local and sell global."

Don't skimp on communications tools. The money you save by not having an easily accessible location for your shop means you must reach out for customers and be easily reached by them. The first time you get a bid three days after your competition because you didn't have a fax machine will probably be the last. My brother has found in his cabinetmaking business that the most effective marketing strategy he has is to respond immediately to requests for bids. Fast response often beats out price considerations in our fast-paced, instant-gratification world. Be ready to respond.

Planning, finding and equipping a shop are the most exciting features of starting a professional woodworking business. They are also the most sobering. The day you commit to your business by signing a lease, buying a new tool or quitting your job is a scary one. You'll sit at your desk or lean against your bench and ask yourself the question every new business owner faces: Where will the work, the sales, the commissions and the money come from? The answer is simple: marketing. You should be devoting at least as much time to your marketing plan as you did to designing and putting together your shop. That's the subject of our next chapter.

WHO WILL BUY MY WORK?

A friend of mine who is the CEO of a training company and a career entrepreneur told me that, in his opinion, the reason so many businesses fail is because the owners don't understand the most basic aspect of being in business: You must sell your business and your services all the time. He argues that no matter what business you are in, sales and marketing are your most important activities. The more I work with new and growing businesses, the more I understand the truth in his words. No selling equals no cash flow, and no cash flow means you're out of business. It's as simple as that.

Unfortunately, when I start to talk about sales and marketing, I can almost hear the books slam shut and the internal denial start up. Newly professional woodworkers want to produce beautiful and functional creations and to believe that the world will beat a path to their doors. It's sad when the months go by and such woodworkers find themselves surrounded by their work and broke. This is usually when they frantically call their local newspaper's ad salesman in a desperate attempt to rescue their businesses.

This sad story does not have to happen to you or anyone else. If you learn a few basic marketing skills, budget some time and a little money for marketing, and put together a simple plan for selling your work, you'll do fine. The secret is to start these actions before you are desperate or broke. In fact, knowing who will buy your products and how to reach your market should be the reason you go into the woodworking business. You discover a need and fill it.

Let's assume you are considering becoming a pro. If you already have a shop or business, just pretend that you're starting from day one. Your experience will make the whole process easier if you keep an open mind. The first question you should ask yourself is: Who will buy my work and why?

▼▼▼

KNOW YOUR CUSTOMER

Suppose, like the owner of Kids and Colors, Inc. (see Chapter 2), that you make kids' furniture. Your buyers are probably parents, right? But think for a moment. Your furniture is pretty high quality, which means it's fairly expensive. So your customers are rich parents, right? Well, maybe, but a lot of new parents are not yet earning the income they will as they get older, and they have a lot of bills. So who has the income? Older people like grandparents, and a little research shows that grandparents spend a lot of money on grandchildren. Grandparents have the money, they have the desire and they can appreciate a quality product that may become a family heirloom. This is the beginning of a marketing strategy—understanding who some of your potential customers are.

But are you selling your kid's furniture directly to retail buyers? You're probably selling to store buyers. So who is your customer? The answer is always this: Your customer is the individual who signs the check. Even if you deal with large architectural firms, builders or corporations, your customer is the individual who has the desire and authority to make the decision and spend the money. That's your customer.

The same idea applies to woodworkers selling small items at craft shows, artists trying to establish a relationship with a prestigious gallery or cabinetmakers building custom kitchens. You must determine which people make the decisions and show how your work will enhance their lives and solve their problems.

To get back to our example, you have acquired some valuable information. You know that the people who will buy your furniture are either well off and/or grandparents. This means you must focus on stores that are in certain areas, carry certain product lines and cater to certain groups of people that fit your description. Once you've found that group, you can tell their buyers how your work will appeal to their customers and what you will do to enhance that appeal. And you will make the sale.

UNDERSTANDING HOW THE MARKET DETERMINES WHAT YOU MAKE

Earlier I discussed that business-success cliché, find a need and fill it. Like many clichés, this one has a lot of truth behind it. What it means is your customers decide what you make. You won't have much choice, except if you design and build your own fine-art pieces. And even in this case if the collectors don't like your vision, you won't make a living. Ultimately the decision is not your own.

To some this lack of control may be disheartening. If you are completely dedicated to having no other person involved in your work, I suggest that you remain a hobbyist woodworker. To have an arrogant attitude toward your market will reward you only with indifference or anger, not cash.

Fortunately, the market is huge and contains almost any imaginable need, taste or desire. Unless you have extremely unusual ideas about what you do, you can probably find someone who is interested in your vision. The challenge in creating a product and seeking a market afterward is to find those dedicated buyers. There may not be enough of them to support you.

It is much easier to find a need and fill it. Your product must solve problems, fulfill desires and provide a high level of satisfaction. It must make people feel good about themselves and their decisions to spend money. Much of the process is psychological. An office manager purchasing a wall of multimedia cabinets for a corporate meeting room has a special set of problems: She must get the job done for the right price and with the right look, and the cabinets must function well and satisfy her bosses. Her overriding concern may be satisfying her bosses. The media wall you build may mean an improvement in her status, proof that she can handle certain kinds of projects or help her step up to another level. You're building cabinets but she's thinking about career moves. If you understand the psychological motivation behind the buyer's interest, you'll be far more likely to make the sale.

Let's return to the kids' furniture for a moment. You have a meeting with the buyer for a chain of upscale children's educational toy stores. Success here could mean a lot to the future of your business. What does this buyer want? What problems is he or she facing? How can you address those problems and get the order? If you can answer these types of questions before you walk into this situation, you'll succeed in business.

The answers to these questions are available to anyone who looks for them. Research will ferret them out. The research may involve attending trade shows and seeing what sells, talking to as many people as possible, going into their stores and looking at what they already carry and developing a profile of your customers that tells you as much about them as possible.

Even if you make lawn ornaments in your garage, you can use this process. You must get into the habit of always looking for more information about the people who buy your birdhouses or happy little dwarves. What do they have in common? Do they read similar magazines, attend certain arts festivals, live in a certain kind of neighborhood? The more you know, the easier it will be to find highly motivated buyers. And when you let the market lead you and your product to those buyers, they will be happy to buy from you.

CREATING A CUSTOMER PROFILE

The first step in understanding how the market determines the product is to create a customer profile. If, like most of us, you serve different kinds of customers, you may need to develop several profiles. However, I think you'll find that certain traits will be common to all of them.

We started creating a customer profile for Kids and Colors, Inc., earlier in this chapter by doing some brainstorming. In the process we discovered that we're selling to three groups of customers: store buyers, grandparents and affluent parents. Because Kids and Colors wants to sell in quantity, its primary customer will be the store buyer. It will sell directly to those buyers; however, some of its marketing efforts must be targeted to the store's customers in order to convince the buyers that their customers will want the product line.

In other cases, you may be selling directly to different kinds of customers. In his cabinet shop, my brother Richard sells to both the design professionals who are specifying cabinetry for commercial projects and to homeowners who are upgrading kitchens, baths, libraries and home offices. To a lesser degree he works with custom-home builders. In all three cases, he had to develop a profile of each group so that he understood their priorities and desires. The architect wants exactly what he or she designs or specifies and is not looking for design input (except for the occasional construction detail). The homeowners often want a complete package from design to installation to a complete remodel, including lighting, plumbing, floor finishing, etc. Richard's ability to offer a complete package (through the use of experienced subcontractors) often means getting the job and increasing his profits. The builders with whom he works are concerned about different things. Time and money are important. Having the cabinets ready to install on-site at the right date can be extremely important. The design is usually part of the house package. In some cases, Richard may have cabinets delivered in a knocked-down state for quick assembly on-site, saving the builder storage and trucking expenses. Knowing these requirements makes the sale possible and profitable.

Decoy carvers or wood turners get to know their market because the places that display and sell their work are usually specialized. They may always deal with a limited number of galleries, gift shops or individual collectors. Once they establish a reputation, their work may be in demand and they may find themselves in the enviable situation of being booked months ahead. This is something that comes from hard work, and some of that work is marketing.

In each of these cases, the woodworkers know their market intimately and are always seeking more information so they can service their customers better. If you are new to woodworking and don't know who will buy your work, it will help to start a customer profile sheet. Do a little brainstorming, jotting down anything you think your prospects will have in common. When brainstorming, the rule is to write down anything that pops out, no matter how absurd. It works because you are, in effect, giving your subconscious permission to work on the problem without interference from your (opinionated) conscious mind.

After brainstorming, talk to other woodworkers, suppliers, store employees and owners, gallery curators, fellow craftspeople and anyone else who might offer insights. Take all strident opinions with a grain of salt since many people will be discouraging or repeat the negative opinions that are keeping them from succeeding. Just take it in and you'll start to recognize the good advice, especially as your experience grows.

You're looking for the following information:

Who buys your work?
Are they males between 35 and 50 with incomes of $60,000+ and homes in a certain suburb? Are they female office managers in midsize manufacturing companies? Or are they retirees who want to attract birds to their garden?

What do they want?
This is a tricky one. Do they want cute birdhouses or birdhouses that attract birds? Do they want a paneled library or the status that such a library may confer? When you discover a specific desire, try to discern the underlying psychological benefit involved. It might be comfort, status, competition and winning, insecurity or a combination of things.

Where are your customers?

Are they located in a specific geographic area such as a wealthy suburb? Or are they united by profession, interest group, hobby or ethnic or religious background? The where determines how you can reach them. If they all read *Audio Video Interiors* magazine or *Home Furniture* magazine, you know a lot about their interests and how to reach them. You can take out an ad or rent a mailing list that targets those specific customers. You can even have lists cross-referenced to filter out members of two or more interests or locations. A combination of certain zip codes and subscribers could lead you to all the AV enthusiasts in your part of the state.

Why do people buy your work?

This is related to what. Knowing why they buy is vital to your success. If you address those concerns you'll be "speaking their language" and establishing rapport—two vital aspects of selling.

When do people buy?

Timing is very important. You won't sell expensive gift items in summer, kitchen projects don't usually happen between Thanksgiving and Christmas and your crafts will probably need to be ready for the show season. Architects, designers and builders operate on tight schedules, and your ability to meet those schedules dependably can earmark you as a reliable resource. Conversely, failure to take your client's time constraints seriously will destroy your business.

How will they pay?

Make sure the person you are dealing with has the power and the ability to make the decisions and sign the checks. This is very important. We've all wasted time and energy meeting with prospects who don't have the decision-making power or simply can't make decisions. There are people in this world who will praise you, say yes and hold long meetings, all the while having no intention or ability to go ahead with the purchase.

Get to know your customers as partners, friends and fellow enthusiasts. *Networking* is simply another word for getting to know people who can send you work or referrals. You succeed in networking by finding shared interests and looking for mutually beneficial relationships. If they send you work, make an effort to send them work. At some point in your career you'll start to meet people who can send you a lot of business. Meeting and developing relationships with these key people is the ultimate marketing goal and the reason for starting to build a customer profile right from the beginning of your professional life. It will help you recognize opportunities and reach out to them.

USING YOUR CUSTOMER PROFILE

The information you gather about the people who will buy your work can be used in many ways. It can help you find new areas of specialization, it can help you target a certain audience for your marketing message and it can help you improve your work (and your profits).

Sometimes one job can lead you into a lucrative new business. A cabinet-maker is asked to fabricate custom rack-mount cabinets for a recording studio. That leads to more studio furniture commissions, and he gradually acquires an expertise and reputation as a studio cabinetry specialist. Capitalizing on the work he's done, he puts together a portfolio showing his studio cabinetry and woodworking business and sends it to the top 20 studio-design firms in the country and to a list of studios in the three-state area where he lives. One connection with one design firm results in enough work to keep his shop busy for an entire year fabricating all the furnishing, cabinets and decorative surfacing for a multi-million dollar facility. Sound too good to be true? Often your marketing is aimed at finding the one individual or connection that can change your business. The more you know about that person, the more likely you are to persuade him or her to do business with you. It's called doing your homework, and it works.

TURNING A HOBBY OR INTEREST INTO A PROFITABLE NICHE

Are you an amateur expert? In other words do you have a hobby that you are immersed in? I'm assuming that hobby has a woodworking aspect to it or you probably wouldn't be reading this book. Your hobby interest represents a great opportunity to start a business because you already know something about the market based on your own exposure to it. Are there people making money doing what you do for fun? If there are, it's a good indication that you too can make the jump. Conversely, if you have a completely unknown and untested idea for a business, I suggest you test the waters carefully before you commit time and money to it. There may be no competition because the idea or product is not viable.

As a hobbyist you read the publications and books available, have some contact with suppliers, and understand the skills and tools required to do woodworking. You should focus on specializing in a profitable niche, learning all you can about marketing and how to price your work to sell so that you make a profit. A birdhouse that takes six hours to construct cannot make money unless you can sell it directly to a customer at a high price (over $100). Add in what a middleman, such as a store, makes with a markup, and you'll need to discount that price by 50% or more. Even if you make $10 an hour you're not making money when you add in overhead, materials and time, not to mention profit.

You can improve these factors by finding ways to spend less time on each piece, by upgrading the piece to command a higher price or by finding another product that will be profitable. Market and pricing knowledge can help you understand these forces before you take the plunge. As a pro, you'll be buying materials in larger quantities and dealing with suppliers at wholesale rates. You'll learn better ways to perform repetitive operations such as cutting out parts and finishing. A new tool might speed up the process. Perhaps you make a birdhouse that matches a neighbor's Victorian house and discover a market for custom (high-priced) birdhouses. One Victorian-house enthusiast sends a picture of your matching birdhouse to *Old-House Journal* and you start getting requests. You run a few ads in the same magazine and suddenly you're in business.

A business like this can grow from a basement bench on the weekend into a full-time company with a catalog, employees and commercial shop space, if that's what you want. You may be more than happy to limit your work to what you can do yourself at home. In that case, you'll restrict your marketing, perhaps generating enough work from word of mouth and some free publicity. These are things you can plan.

▼▼▼

CHOOSING A SPECIALTY

Almost everyone specializes these days, and for several good reasons. In order to get proficient you will need to concentrate your skill building on a few areas. While an instrument maker may be capable of making a cabinet, he would have to decide whether he wouldn't prefer to stay focused on the lengthy process of learning his chosen craft. Specialization also pays better and is easier to sell without resorting to lowball bids and prices. This is because we recognize that experts may cost more but they save time and have knowledge and skills that get the job done right. When you hire experts, you are tapping into their entire accumulated knowledge and experience. This makes their time more valuable to you.

When you are a specialist, you can offer your services to other woodworkers when you have the extra time. If you specialize in painted finishes it may pay for a local cabinet shop to farm out that part of a job to you because it doesn't have to invest in training and tools for what may be an unusual commission. Your work is marked up and everybody profits. Specialization also means that you may come to be known as what I call a "local expert." Local experts are recognized authorities on whatever their specialty is. You can turn yourself into one by using publicity to tell the world about your interest. If you do a good job, you'll become the first person anyone thinks of calling when it comes to your area of expertise.

Specialties can be process related, service related or product related. Processes are things such as carving, finishing, turning, joinery, veneer work, etc. Services include installation, design work, consulting, contracting and supplying specialty items such as hardware. Product-related specialties include cabinetmaking, furnituremaking, product lines, moldings, church work, craft items and any other products in which you specialize.

The possibilities for specialization are enormous, and there are woodworkers who do well with obscure niches. One of my favorites is a woodworker in my building who carves chin rests for violins. They're made to fit the violinist, and he commands pretty good prices for this unusual specialty. It helps that our city has a major music school and that classical violinists think nothing of spending $25,000 on an instrument, $2,500 on a bow and $500 on a case. (All made by specialist woodworkers!)

I'd recommend starting out with a variety of skills and letting your market show you the potentially profitable specialty areas. Like the cabinetmaker who became an expert on recording-studio furnishings, your customers can point the way to a lucrative woodworking niche. It is not unusual to have several specialties that use related skills and tools.

The big advantage of specialization for a beginning professional woodworker is that it allows you to ease into the business, and it helps you differentiate yourself from your more experienced competition. While your area may not need another custom furnituremaker, there may be a call for someone who specializes in home-theater furniture. Is there a difference in the skills you need? Not a significant one. However, as a specialist you'll get to know the special requirements, the suppliers and resources that cater to that niche, and you'll know how to talk knowledgeably with other pros in that field, such as designers and audio salespeople. If you and the general custom-furniture shop are bidding the job, you'll have the edge because of your expertise.

Knowing your customers enables you to target those customers and their needs. Targeting ensures that your marketing dollars work effectively. Specializing in one or more fields makes it easy to target your customers, to tell the world about your business and to define yourself as unique and valuable. And that means more profits from more interesting work. One of the secrets of marketing a small business when you have a limited budget is to focus on the optimum market for your specialty. Because we live in a large, diverse world with easy long-distance communication, you can prosper as a specialist, serving the needs of a select group of specially targeted and highly motivated customers, wherever you are located. The first step to achieving that goal is to know your customer.

GARY MEIXNER AND PITTSFORD LUMBER: FROM THE SUPPLIER SIDE

The suppliers you deal with daily are resources and potential partners in the success of your woodworking business. As a professional your material and tool needs are going to be different from those of a hobbyist, and the places you go to fill those needs will be different from the local lumberyard or home center.

Gary Meixner works at a company that supports and supplies a large number of serious woodworkers and offers its own specialized woodshop facilities. Pittsford Lumber and Woodshop is a hardwood lumber dealer; a supplier of esoteric tools from Japanese saws to specialized carving knives; a woodworking shop offering custom woodwork to local manufacturers and a pretty good place to pick up advice, referrals and

gossip. Gary is one of a group of woodworkers who run the company and work in the shop and the yard. He has been a professional woodworker for over 20 years, including stints as a furniture restorer, a carpenter, a furnituremaker and now as an all-around expert on the supply side of the woodworking business.

Pittsford Lumber inhabits the few remaining buildings of a turn-of-the-century lumberyard in a scenic town along New York's Erie Canal. As we talked we were surrounded by stacks of black walnut and oak, racks of chisels and woodworking books, parts, hardware and an ongoing dialogue between Gary's partners and a steady stream of customers. The environment was saturated with the smells, sights and sounds of the woodworking business.

I asked Gary about the differences between the needs of a pro woodworker and those of the amateurs who also support his business. His answers were a combination of business advice and a reserved judgment on the potential for success in a tough business.

About half of his clientele are professionals, and that includes everyone who dips into woodworking as a professional, including carpenters, hobbyists with an occasional commission, full-time shops and new businesses. His yard gets a cross section because they sell smaller quantities of lumber, do some custom milling and shaping and they are easy to deal with one on one. Gary noted that large shops seldom buy from them because they are not price competitive on large orders and don't offer delivery services. However, the buyer can come in and look the wood over before buying.

Like most suppliers, a pro can open a credit account by filling out a credit application. In Gary's experience as a shop owner, he found that opening accounts and developing good credit often made the difference when he faced a need to buy large quantities of materials at the beginning of a job. It also helps establish your business as a legitimate company with a track record.

(continued)

Once suppliers know and trust a woodworker's track record there is a good chance that they will pass on requests for referrals that come in from local people and companies needing professional woodworking services. Gary said that they were hesitant to recommend any woodworker or shop that they didn't trust completely, a strong reason why any referral should be treated with extra care. The individual or company that makes a referral is putting its reputation in your hands.

Gary's advice for success in this business echoed that of most of the pros with whom I talked. He advised developing a specialty and seeking niche markets. In particular he said to be careful about the specialty you choose, making sure that there is a profitable market for it. He learned about it the hard way.

Earlier in Gary's career, he worked on Long Island as a restorer of expensive Colonial furniture. The area had the history and economy to guarantee a large number of pieces to work on and collectors with the deep pockets required to support such specialized work. When Gary moved upstate he started a similar business only to find that the history of the area began later and most of the local antiques were machine-age furniture, which was not only a different specialty but a market that could seldom afford expensive restoration work. His change in location meant a big change in the market and the failure of that part of his woodworking business.

Pittsford Lumber supplies a large number of part-time and serious hobbyist woodworkers, including several who have made the leap from hobbyist to pro. Based on their experiences, Gary also suggested considering a specialty that doesn't require a large financial commitment to tools and shop space. He mentioned carving and turning as two disciplines that require more skill than money. By keeping costs down, focusing on craft, building a reputation for expertise and quality and servicing a niche market, you can gradually build a successful woodworking business.

Finally, Gary had an interesting idea of what constitutes success in the woodworking world. He felt that you must be able to net at least $30,000 a year to consider yourself successful. In his experience, any less meant that you weren't earning an income comparable to other similar professions. He also voiced a common complaint about new shop owners who enter the market setting their prices so low that other shops couldn't possibly compete. In his experience, while these lowball shops seldom last more than a year, they will always be around making life harder for the pricier (and more realistic) competition. He sincerely hopes that people contemplating entering the woodworking business will look realistically at what they must charge. Both his business and those of his customers suffer when new shops fail because of unrealistic pricing and shoddy work.

CHAPTER 7

HOW MUCH MONEY DO I NEED?

"It takes money to make money."

We've all heard the saying, and in our capitalist society it is often true that you need capital to get a business up and running. In the woodworking world you have two choices. You can invest money in your business with the intention of getting a return in the form of profits. The money may come from savings, loans from family, bank loans or a number of sources. If you plan well, your start-up capital will be adequate to set up your business and keep it running until you begin receiving the cash flow that is the lifeblood of any business.

The other option is to start from scratch and use what resources you have to get things flowing. This approach, called *bootstrapping* because it involves pulling yourself up by your own bootstraps, is best for the part-time business. You can start a woodworking business in a corner of a basement or garage, with a few tools and your skills.

Money is a sensitive issue with new businesses. Many woodworkers I know are uncomfortable admitting that it is an important part of being a professional. The approach you take to the money that flows through your business will, to a great extent, determine how much enjoyment you get out of the business. Learn about it now, and you'll seldom have to worry about it later.

INVESTING IN YOUR FUTURE

Money is a powerful tool. It is more powerful than any table saw or shaper. Money is a representation of accumulated energy and time. You put 20 hours into a piece of furniture and receive a payment that includes a certain number of dollars for your skills and time. Because money is a very sophisticated and powerful tool, using it requires training and skill. A big part of being in business involves learning and applying those money skills.

Money never disappears unless it is stolen, and even then, a savvy money manager has anticipated the possibility and used some form of insurance to protect the business. Money management and planning are essential for helping you increase the value of your money (your time and skill) and invest it wisely to receive a good return.

When you start your business you often have to make many investments that take time to show you a return. Tools, rent, insurance, office equipment and marketing are some of the possibilities. No matter how painful the investment may seem, if you work hard, it will pay you back many times over. You don't spend money to start a business, you invest money in your future. This attitude and approach is vital if you are going to succeed. Try to consider the long-term return on your investment when you put money into your woodworking company.

Capital expenditures are investments in the long-term success of your business. These include tools, real estate, product development, start-up marketing efforts and any other initial investment in a tangible lasting aspect of your business.

Overhead is the ongoing cost of doing business, including rent, utilities, supplies, insurance, regular marketing expenses like Yellow Pages ads, labor and professional services. Materials and inventory are the raw materials and finished products that you have on hand.

Each of these areas requires an investment, especially when you're starting a new business or making the leap from part-timer to full time. We're going to look at those investments that are considered start-up investments and those that are ongoing investments or overhead. Before we can get into that, we have to take a look at accounting.

Accounting and bookkeeping are skills you must learn to succeed. It is not necessary to become a numbers whiz or spend hours struggling through accounting classes (although taking classes can be an illuminating experience). There are several bookkeeping software programs available that will handle nearly any need you may have. Most of them are as simple as a checkbook and have the added advantage of producing professional-looking invoices and tracking them. If you don't have a computer you can get a simple one-write system at an office supply store and have your accountant show you how to set it up. An hour or two of simple book-keeping per week will keep most woodworking businesses running.

In case you are wondering, there are several compelling reasons for getting your act together moneywise from the beginning. It helps you keep Uncle Sam happy while making sure that you are taking full advantage of the many tax benefits that owning a business can offer. You definitely need an accountant for this, particularly one who is experienced in working with small businesses. The equipment, supplies, utility bills and labor charges you pay are deductible at different rates and over various lengths of time. You'll want to be able to take full advantage of this.

Another important feature of accounting is its role as an information system. This is especially true when you use a software product to track the flow of money through your business. Your computer can instantly generate profit-and-loss statements, expense statements for specific projects or products and many other useful reports. This capability becomes handy when bidding a job that is similar to one you've done in the past or when pricing a new product. Your profit-and-loss statement also tells you whether you made money on a project and may help you spot areas where you can do better.

Learn enough about accounting to get a system working for you. *Small-Time Operator* by Bernard Kamaroff (see Resources on p. 150) is an excellent start-up guide for those of you who can't handle the numbers.

▼▼▼

A START-UP BUDGET WORKSHEET

Let's take a look at a typical start-up budget for a woodworker who is beginning a full-time business in a rented shop. You can adapt this to your requirements to get a good idea of what you should have on hand as start-up capital. Some of these expenses can be avoided by putting in more of your own time and effort, which is known as "sweat equity" and is another way of spending energy instead of cash. Remember that it sometimes pays to have others do what they do best while you focus on your strengths. If it takes you 40 hours to wire your shop and an electrician 10, you might be using your resources more efficiently to pay him and focus your efforts on something at which you are skilled. If you simply don't have the money, you must make the time. Remember that you may be taking time away from your woodworking, which brings in the money.

START-UP BUDGET

Living expenses
Often forgotten is that you must pay your living expenses while you're starting your business. If you work part time and have another job or a spouse who can temporarily support you, fine. Otherwise you will need three to six months' living expenses to see you through until the money starts coming in. Even if you take on several big projects right away, you may not see any profits for a few months. You need a cushion. Figure three to six times your current monthly take-home pay.

If you live lavishly or are heavily in debt, it may not be advisable to leave an income-producing job and start a business. Start paring down your bills and paying off your debts. It's good practice for running a business to eliminate unnecessary luxuries and expenses at home before you are dependent on the sometimes uneven income experienced by an entrepreneur. Paying off your credit cards also gives you a fallback source of revolving credit for your business in the future.

Deposits
You'll be putting up money for security deposits on your rent, utilities and phone. This, unfortunately, is money you probably won't see again for the life of your business, unless you can negotiate its return in the future, after you have proven your trustworthiness. Since this initial outlay can amount to several thousand dollars, I recommend negotiating the best possible deal to reduce these deposits before you sign any agreements.

Capital investments and improvements
Any building, renovating, rewiring, painting, etc., that you must do to get your doors open is considered a capital improvement. Remember when budgeting for these things that commercial requirements are different from residential ones. You will likely be required by law to have licensed contractors do the work or at least inspect it, particularly when it comes to electrical, plumbing and HVAC (heating, ventilation and air conditioning). You may also be looking at installing dust removal and air ventilation systems for finishing, explosion-proof fans, safe storage areas for chemicals and many other required expenses. Plan ahead and budget for them after you talk to local building-code officials about what is needed.

Tools
When you're starting out, go slowly with tool purchases until you know what you'll need, especially when it comes to major expenditures on big power tools. Get the basics, and buy the exotic tools as you need them or when they will obviously make a worthwhile contribution to your operation. Don't underestimate the cost of hand tools and hand power tools.

When my brother and I did an inventory of his shop prior to a move, we were surprised to find that his hand tools added up to a greater investment than his large stationary power tools.

Your accountant will be writing off your tools, over time. You may not, in many cases, write off a big tool all at once. The tax law says that such a tool has a usable life span of three to five years, and you may only write off a percentage of its value each year. Check with your accountant if you are planning on tax write-offs to help pay your tool expenses (as you should be).

Starting inventory

Materials such as wood, finishes, glue and sandpaper; equipment such as saw blades, drill and router bits; office supplies and any other purchases that you consume are significant start-up expenses because you may be financing your starting inventories of these items. It is amazing what a seemingly insignificant item such as sandpaper can cost over a year of full-time woodworking. Once you get rolling these things become part of your overhead and production costs. Now, at the start, you must take them into consideration when budgeting.

Marketing costs

Start-up is the time to plan your marketing and provide an adequate budget for it. It is easy to become involved in shop remodeling and tool purchases and not leave any cash for promoting yourself. In my opinion, it is far more important to put aside more money and time for marketing than for tool purchases. Once customers start giving you deposits for projects or start ordering bookcases, you can buy the tools you need. There is nothing more depressing than sitting in a beautiful, well-equipped shop with nothing to do while the bills keep piling up.

To budget your marketing costs you need a simple plan for your first year's marketing. That plan probably calls for some kind of informational brochure or sell sheet and methods for getting it out to likely customers. Putting together such a marketing piece is one of the significant investments you must make when starting your business. By getting it done in the beginning, you'll have a valuable tool you can use to generate business for your shop. Other necessary marketing tools are business cards, letterhead and envelopes with your company name and logo on them. In Chapters 8 and 9 we'll go into your marketing plan and budget in detail.

Insurance

There are several kinds of insurance you'll need from the beginning. Theft, fire and disaster insurance protects your investment in your business, health insurance protects you from medical bills and disability insurance covers the loss of income-earning ability should you get injured. Some clients may expect some kind of bond or project-completion insurance. You'll also need liability insurance to protect yourself from injury lawsuits arising from accidents involving your work or shop. Proof of adequate liability insurance may be required when submitting competitive bids. Having liability insurance may help you win a bid over one from an uninsured competitor. An insurance broker with small-business experience can guide you through the options. Use a well-known company.

One final tip about insurance. Get a high deductible to save on premiums. It may be cheaper to pay out-of-pocket for small (under $1,000) losses than to pay the higher rates that low deductibles mean. If you can't afford the cost of full health insurance, there is a tactic that can protect you from major medical bills that could mean the loss of your business: There are health-insurance policies with very large deductibles ($5,000 for instance). They are much cheaper and, in essence, mean you pay all your noncatastrophic medical expenses out-of-pocket while keeping protection for major medical bills. Having this minimum insurance is far better than going without health insurance.

Education

Both woodworking and running a small business are highly skilled activities. You may want to invest in training through taking college courses or seminars, reading and going to conferences and trade shows. This start-up investment can mean long-term savings of thousands of dollars. Try to budget money for subscriptions to trade magazines, new books and other educational materials that can increase your business and craft skills. Join local business and trade associations and be an active member. The small dues payments can mean a lot of work over the years as you make connections and build a reputation.

The amount of money required for starting up can be daunting; however, you are investing in your future and the American dream of succeeding on your own. This investment may determine your earning ability and quality of life for many years. Doing it right at the beginning can mean being profitable early in your business life and remaining so. Undercapitalization is a primary reason for the many failures of new small businesses.

AN OPERATING BUDGET WORKSHEET (OVERHEAD)

Overhead is the regular cost of doing business. It includes all those bills you pay monthly, office supplies and labor costs. You would also include any regular amount of time and money you devote each month to marketing your business. Overhead may include loan payments, insurance payments and other regular expenses. Overhead is the minimum amount of cash you need to survive on a monthly or weekly basis. Ultimately, if you're only meeting your expenses you're not succeeding as a business. Profit is the measure of financial success.

If you understand what your overhead is, you can derive a figure for your "shop rate," which is an hourly figure you can use when doing estimates and bids. Your shop rate is your hourly overhead plus a percentage for profit. It's useful for quoting your minimum rate when people ask you to do small jobs. It also helps when you are pricing product lines or things you are making in quantity. And if you get really busy and the market justifies it, you can raise your shop rate, increasing your profits.

Shop rate is important because many inexperienced woodworkers undercharge because they don't understand the relationship between overhead and profit. It is very likely that the woodworker who charges $15 an hour for a project is losing money or at best breaking even. This is because when you are in business for yourself you can't think in terms of what you would settle for as a salary. Your actual take-home pay is only a part of what you must charge if you want to succeed.

The following example will walk you through the process of establishing a shop rate. I've kept it as simple as possible but you'll have to adapt it to your situation. Different skill levels, geographic areas and other considerations will have a significant impact on your shop rate. For these reasons, you should work out your own shop rate rather than relying on some kind of average figure. Start with monthly bills (see the chart below).

ESTABLISHING A SHOP RATE

rent (or a percentage of your mortgage payment or rent if you work at home)	$ 300.00
utilities	200.00
phone	75.00
miscellaneous supplies	75.00
insurance	100.00
postage, gas, shipping	50.00
loan payment	200.00
salary (160 hours @$15 per hour)	2,400.00
marketing	100.00
other	100.00
total overhead/per month	$3,600.00
or per hour ($3,600/160 hours)	22.50
add 20% profit	+ 4.50
shop rate	$ 27.00

This shop rate is the basis for estimating your work. You'll notice that materials are not included. They must be estimated separately because they vary greatly from project to project or are based on the quantity of a product you are making. Always remember to add on a markup or profit to any materials you sell a buyer, including hardware and outsourced components. This markup covers your time and effort in procuring the materials.

HOW MUCH TO PAY YOURSELF

You'll notice that I picked a number as salary for the example of $15 per hour. Your choice of what to pay yourself, aside from profit, should be based on what you would have to pay a comparably skilled worker in your marketplace. If your competitors are paying their workers $5 an hour and you pay yourself $15, your bids won't be competitive. You must be realistic.

CASH FLOW AND PROFITS

I've mentioned cash flow and profits several times. I waited to provide definitions of these key money concepts because I knew they would be clearer after I walked you through some of the money considerations. Cash flow has been described as the lifeblood of any business. It is the flow of money through a business that pays the bills, buys the improvements and keeps things running. A business can be successful and still have cash-flow problems because of late payments from customers or the necessity to provide up-front funding for a big project. For this reason and others, cash flow is one of the main things that a bank looks at when considering a loan application. A business that is only marginally profitable but has a steady cash flow is more likely to pay its bills regularly and stay afloat than a business that makes big money erratically.

Keeping your cash flow steady can be hard when you're waiting 90 days for a final payment on a big commercial project. For this reason, many woodworkers will be willing to take work that isn't particularly profitable in order to pay the bills. Often, developing a product line on the side can help with cash-flow problems even if the products aren't very profitable.

As an entrepreneur, you'll receive profits as your reward for owning your business (or you'll have to absorb losses). Profits come from marking up your prices to reflect your value-added expertise and skill. These profits may be reinvested in your business to help ensure its growth, to update tools or equipment or to increase your marketing effectiveness. Or you may pocket them, or do a little of everything. If you have a good year, you'll want to consult your accountant and/or a financial planner to determine the best action to take.

Building a profitable business is the most common route to wealth in our society. A recent survey of the thousands of millionaires in the United States revealed that the average millionaire owns a comfortable but unpretentious home, has normal spending habits and is the owner of a small to midsize manufacturing company. If you ever decide to sell your woodworking business, your profits may well be the major determinant of the sale price.

▼ ▼ ▼

ESTIMATES AND QUOTES

Pricing your work is one of the most daunting tasks facing the newly professional woodworker. This is particularly true when you are bidding competitively against other woodworkers. The only way to handle these situations is to estimate the job at the price you can afford and take your chances. There will always be companies that will drastically underbid work, and getting into a price war with them is a waste of time. Once you get a reputation for being the cheapest guy in town, your customers will always expect rock-bottom prices, and the customers interested in good quality will go elsewhere. Stick to your price and don't spend a lot of energy worrying about jobs that got away. The work you lowball always tends to be the biggest headache. (This could be called the Murphy's law of self-employment.)

You'll be faced with the decision to quote a price or an hourly rate. In general, I recommend an hourly rate for repair jobs or situations where you won't know what you're getting into until you're there. For very small jobs, most shops have a minimum, usually two hours at shop rate. Doing $20 jobs is not worth the effort unless you have nothing else to do. If you're working hourly, you can quote your shop rate. Try to stick to it.

In general, it is always preferable to give a total quote for a project. Large projects are a challenge, but eventually you'll know when you're in the ballpark. Until you've made enough bids to do them with confidence, you can use the following list to develop a method that will work for you.

1. Using your shop rate, divide the job into tasks and calculate how long it will take you to do each task. Don't forget to include time spent in meetings, on the phone, tracking down materials and suppliers and something extra for unexpected problems. Total the hours and multiply by your shop rate.

2. Calculate your total materials cost and add 15% to 20% for a markup to cover your resourcefulness. Remember you can get better prices than a walk-in consumer and have access to more suppliers. Give yourself a profit on the items you resell to a customer. Shop supplies such as glue and sandpaper are built into the shop rate, unless you will be using an unusually large amount, in which case you may want to add them to your materials cost. When you order materials, be sure to account for the large amount of waste resulting from the work. Anyone who has milled rough lumber knows that at least as 50% or more of what you buy ends up as scrap or sawdust. Also there will be a certain amount of unusable material caused by checking, discoloration, warp, etc.

3. Total your shop time and materials and consider the number. This is where experience and your personal assessment of the situation come in. If you are much higher than the range the customer wanted, you must either cut your price or scale down some phase of the job. In general, it is always a good idea to stick to your price if customers balk and show them places where they can cut corners by reducing the amount of work or features put into the project. Lowering your price without changing the project will undermine your credibility.

4. Type out a professional-looking quote that is straightforward, clearly written and has all the information the customer wants. Potential problem areas should be clearly spelled out with a method for dealing with them. These include change orders, mistakes in design that are not your fault and any other unexpected problems. The quote can be on a form that becomes a contract when signed by the customer and you. It should clearly spell out a completion time, terms for payment and what is included. Use your letterhead and be professional. These forms are available as two-part Quote/Contract forms at any office-supply store. You can use the format and boilerplate language from these forms for your customized estimate or use the generic ones. Type, stamp or write your business information on them.

5. Present the quote to your customers and make sure it is clear to them. Don't apologize or start explaining your prices. In this situation, the first person to make an excuse or concession is the loser. If they are happy make sure they sign the quote. Usually your terms will be to start the job upon receiving the signed quote and a deposit.

Although it is hard to say no to work, there are situations when it is more professional to stick to your guns. If you feel that your price will be too high for a particular customer, you must decide if you want to do the work for less before you present your price. Don't start any job without a signed contract and deposit, if required.

Preparing and presenting bids is part of the overall sales and marketing operation. You'll learn a great deal by listening carefully to the customer's desires and needs during your initial meeting. Take some notes, defining any "hot"-button topics your customers emphasize. Make sure you address those concerns in the bid. If your bid proposes solutions to their specific problems you have a far better chance to win the job than you would with a cheap price and superficial bid that didn't address their concerns. Good salesmanship can mean more money on each job.

Product lines have a different set of criteria when it comes to pricing. We'll look at pricing a product in detail in Chapter 10.

▼▼▼

EMPLOYEES

At some point you may need help to run your business profitably. The decision to hire an employee or employees is a big one because of the responsibility it entails. When you hire someone you are agreeing to provide him or her with work and pay, whether you have that work or not, unless they are temp workers or subcontractors. If they are subcontractors, you cannot, by law, ask them to show up at certain hours or work for an hourly wage. Before you work with a subcontractor, be sure to review the laws with your accountant and lawyer. If you violate the legal description of a subcontractor relationship you may be liable for back taxes, withholding, worker's compensation and other deductions you should have taken.

Temporary employees work for an agency that takes care of all their payroll and insurance needs. You contract with the agency for their workers. While it sounds ideal, it is expensive and you will discover that it's difficult to obtain skilled workers.

Permanent employees are people in whom you invest a considerable sum with the hope that the work they do will more than justify the cost of having them. Your expense is not just monetary. You must train them and provide a safe environment and various perks, including medical insurance, vacations, etc. Because they are an investment, the decision to take on employees is based on need. If a helper can save you more time and money than it costs you to hire him, then you may be making a justifiable business decision. If you are a loner who likes to make your own hours without being beholden to anyone, an employee may be too much of a burden.

The wage you pay a worker is based on the prevailing rates in your area, his or her skill level and the availability of good-quality people. You'll have to try out a wage and see if you can attract the skill level you need. You can use part-timers, college students or even an intern from a local trade school. Using part-timers is a way to try out an employee before making a commitment to bring on someone full time.

Payroll also includes Social Security withholding, worker's compensation insurance and other withholdings required by state and federal laws. You must withhold taxes and document your actions. For a small-business owner, the paperwork can be overwhelming. Fortunately there are payroll companies that will handle all the paperwork for a small monthly fee. For most small businesses, the expense is more than worth it, since payroll companies save you time and help you avoid legal and taxation hassles. Look under Payroll in the Yellow Pages.

▼ ▼ ▼

RETURN ON INVESTMENT

Throughout our discussion about the role of money in your woodworking business, I've emphasized return on investment. Your money should always be earning interest in one form or another. If it sits still, inflation eats away at it, reducing your net worth and the value of your labor. The money you invest in your business helps you earn a living, builds an asset that you can sell or pass on to others, and provides jobs and other benefits for society. It's important to keep an eye on how well your investment is performing, whether it is invested in a piece of machinery, a brochure or training an employee. You should realize a gain from all of your dollars. Your accounting system and your accountant can help you to track both the tangible and intangible gains (or losses) you are realizing.

At times you may have substantial sums of cash on hand. Good money management means making sure that these short-term cash hoards earn money while you have them whether you sweep them into a money-market account or use a cash-management account that automatically does this for you. Make sure it is a "no-load" account (without excess fees). You may also want to talk to a certified financial planner to arrange to put a portion of your profits to work for your retirement. As a business owner you are entitled to various tax-deferred investment strategies that can make a difference in your economic situation for years to come. Be sure to start taking advantage of them early in the life of your business. Every year of investment has an impact on your overall return later.

Money is of major importance in being a profitable, professional woodworker. It is a significant measure of your success and can mean the difference between long-term comfort and mere survival. Become knowledgeable and skilled at money management, make good use of your expert team members and keep up-to-date with your books and you'll succeed. Ignore money matters and you may find yourself wondering what happened to your once-pleasurable business.

CHAPTER 8

BUILDING A PORTFOLIO AND A REPUTATION

*Your business name
and identity*

*Business cards
and stationery*

Your portfolio

Marketing materials

Telling the world

Throughout the first half of this book I've focused on what it takes to get your woodworking business started, including setting it up, planning your shop and financing the whole endeavor. All of these actions are vital, but they will not help you succeed if the world doesn't know who you are. You need paying customers for your work.

As a new business owner, you may not have any reputation preceding you. You can view this either as a handicap or, as I prefer, as an advantage. No one has preconceived notions about who you are, what you can do or how much you charge. You have a clean slate. If you have been working as a woodworker and want to be more successful or make a transition to a different kind of woodworking, now is the time to start. The marketing strategies and tactics covered in the next two chapters will help you.

This chapter could be titled "The ABCs of Marketing." Like the ABCs, you need to master the basics to take advantage of the more complex components of marketing yourself. Get them right now, at the beginning, and you'll profit more and sooner. You'll also find out that marketing can be one of the most interesting tasks involved in being in business for yourself. It has been compared to an infinitely variable game with very concrete rewards, and there is no reason why anyone cannot master it.

YOUR BUSINESS NAME AND IDENTITY

When you start your business, relatively few people know who you are or what you can do. However, as soon as you start your business, the word starts spreading via friends, relatives, suppliers, your landlord, your lawyer, your insurance agent and anyone else with whom you've had contact during your start-up. This word of mouth may last for a few moments or may grow and spread, depending on your actions in the beginning.

Ultimately, all sales come from word of mouth. Joe buys a TV from the new discount store and tells his buddies while they're watching the big game. The next time they want to buy a new TV, they'll think of Joe and his TV. This word of mouth is encouraged and reinforced by advertising, publicity, mailings, articles in the media, networking and all the other techniques that make up the world of marketing. The first step you can take to keep your reputation and the initial word of mouth alive is to create a memorable identity for your business.

By identity, I mean company name; any visual image attached to that name, such as a logo; any further description of what you do, such as a tag line; and the ways these components are communicated to the world. For instance, your name can say a lot about what you do, or it can confuse everyone or turn people off. You can choose a compelling and memorable image to go with that name, or you can use a little picture of a man with a hammer and saw that your printer offers for free. You can answer your phone with a mumbled greeting, or you can clearly identify yourself and offer your assistance. You can send out an estimate clearly typed on good-quality letterhead that shows you are established and reliable, or you can send a scribbled note on a piece of legal paper.

These comparisons show how simple approaches that cost little can make a big difference in how you are perceived by the customer. If I receive a scribbled quote for a job, I assume it will be a low bid, but I also consider whether I can rely on that company to complete the job. A few dollars' investment in stationery and a word processor might have saved the bid.

The name of your business must be memorable, easy to say and remember, somewhat descriptive and unique in your sphere of influence. Gauzowski Woodworking might not get a call from an embarrassed caller who is afraid of mispronouncing it. The caller won't get it right when he or she makes a referral either. The name will lose the company work. Big Oak Woodworking, on the other hand, is simple, descriptive and memorable. It would be the perfect name in most communities. In my town there is a golf range called Big Oak that advertises all over and will protect its name, even from an unrelated business. Here it wouldn't work. A little research can help you avoid picking a name already in use by another local company.

If you use your own name, you can use a descriptive tag line to reinforce your identity. You might be Johnson Smith, Handturned Burlwood Bowls. Using your own name is recommended when you are trying to build a reputation as an artist/craftsperson. The collectors who purchase your work are probably interested in your personal stature.

Made-up names give you the opportunity to create a feeling in the minds of your customers about the quality of your work. A name like Sycamore Green Kitchen Cabinetry may conjure up images of expansive, shady lawns and a comfortable, affluent lifestyle. If this would appeal to your target customers, then it's a good choice. A company creating a product line may want a brand name that they can build on and market for years to come. Kids and Colors, Inc., serves as both a company name and the brand name for their line of children's furniture. It has the added advantage of cementing their image as the makers of the highly colorful furniture your kids love.

Try some potential names and tag lines on friends and business acquaintances to see how they react, which ones people remember and what kind of message the suggestions convey about your business. Any negative reaction should be carefully considered. Once you have a name, you need a logo or a consistent way of displaying the name on your stationery and marketing materials. Logos are visual symbols of your company and will be remembered because most people recall images as well as words. If you can afford one, use an experienced graphic designer to create your logo. If you can't afford a good designer, don't use the work of an artistic friend. Rather than an amateur effort, you'll be better off with a nicely designed typeface logo put together for much less money by the same designer. Add a tag line and have the designer create a business card, letterhead and envelope package. Get your stationery printed and make sure it contains all your contact information, including address, phone, fax, e-mail, home phone and anything else that will make it easy for someone to reach you.

▼▼▼

BUSINESS CARDS AND STATIONERY

Your business card serves as a set of contact information for your customers. It will get filed in their rotary files for future reference, serve as a reminder of past conversations or casual meetings, work as a mini brochure and help keep your business in the minds of your customers. Hand out your cards freely, even if you've given someone one before. Attach them to outgoing mail, including bill payments. You never know where a potential customer may come upon it. Offer them at the start of any meeting, and you'll get one in return. When you get back to your office, put the cards you've received into your customer database or file.

As I mentioned earlier, professional stationery might mean beating out a less competent-looking competitor in a bid situation. It may also get you in the door, particularly with commercial customers, designers and other visually sophisticated people. Since good-quality stationery implies that you are established and reliable, it will especially impress customers such as homeowners, who may be writing you a very large deposit check for kitchen cabinets or a piece of custom furniture.

You can run your printed stationery through a laser printer and create professional-looking lists, product-information sheets and other inexpensive marketing materials. Stationery can be used for press releases, invoices and order forms. You might have better luck collecting past-due debts if your collection letter is printed on official-looking stationery.

Your goal when using cards and stationery should be to get them out and working for you. Don't hold back the "good" letterhead and envelopes. They serve as inexpensive roaming advertisements for your business, particularly if they display a compelling name, logo and tag line.

Once you have an established name and logo, or if you plan on soliciting business statewide or nationally, I recommend that you have your attorney register your name as a trademark. Do this before you invest in advertising and you won't have to worry about another company getting a court order requiring you to stop using a name that is similar to theirs. Your name can become an important and valued business asset. A good name may increase the value of your company in a sale and/or help you to get and keep business.

▼ ▼ ▼

YOUR PORTFOLIO

Making a name for yourself is different from making up a name. As a craftsperson, you will ultimately be recognized by your work, not only the work you do, but also whom you've done it for, on what scale and how successfully. All of these things comprise your portfolio. A portfolio is a record of your work, a presentation tool used in sales and marketing, and it helps demonstrate design concepts, display styles and finishes and shows your ability to complete projects. If you create products for manufacture, your portfolio is likely to be a catalog or sell sheet. A sell sheet is a one-page marketing piece that shows a product, includes its specs and ordering information and does a little selling. A folder full of sell sheets becomes the portfolio of a larger manufacturing woodworking company.

As a woodworker newly turned professional, your portfolio may be skimpy or filled with work you've done as a hobbyist or student. There may be pieces you completed as an employee working for another woodshop. Because your source material is scarce, you must choose only your best work, and you must try to photograph everything you do to add to your book. If you are creating a product line, you'll need to build samples and prototypes for marketing and demonstrations. A cabinet shop may need to fabricate a wall or roomful of cabinetry to serve as a display and sales tool and serve as their portfolio.

Although every portfolio may not be a notebook full of 8x10 glossies, it is essential to put together some kind of demonstration of your work. The classic portfolio is a notebook filled with excellent-quality photos of your work. Most woodworkers have something like this, and it is definitely worth your time and effort to assemble one. Show your best work. Use detail shots to showcase craftsmanship and features that you offer, including finishes, various woods and hardware, veneers, etc. These shots can beef up a thin start-up portfolio. Even if you have a large selection of work, narrow it down to the pieces that best represent the kind of work you want to do. Even more important, tailor your portfolio to the interests of your customer. If you're meeting with someone who needs commercial cabinetry, fill your book with cabinet shots and include only one or two examples of your other work. Use your portfolio as a powerful selling tool.

With today's inexpensive, high-quality color-copying processes you have another option. Have 20 full-color copies of the top 10 photos in your portfolio made. Your local office-supply store probably carries hard plastic portfolio binders with plastic sleeves designed to hold 12 to 16 pages. They run around $4 each. Buy 20 and make up 20 portfolios. Include a fact sheet on your letterhead, a recent-projects sheet detailing past customers (with their permission), the projects and the problems each solved. Include some business cards and you have an extremely effective sales tool. The total investment for 20 portfolios is about $350, or $17.50 each. If you can't afford all 20 at once, make up as many as you can.

These portfolios go to customers who have the potential to send you repeat business, who can make referrals or who can hand the portfolios on to others. Most successful custom woodshops work with a relatively small number of customers. Spending $20 on each of the key contacts is worth the expense, and I guarantee they won't forget who you are.

The advantages of this tactic are that your portfolio is impressive enough to avoid the circular file (wastebasket), it will be kept for reference and you can update it for regular customers. Save a few extras to leave with good prospects. You can send them out with return postage included when dealing with distant customers. This is a common practice with professional photographers, who always keep several portfolios ready to drop into the mail. UPS will even sell you a return label that your customer can slap on the package and hand to the UPS driver. It has a code that routes the package to you with no addressing required.

Soon you may be putting your portfolio or catalog onto a CD-ROM, a World Wide Web site on the Internet or sending out a video. These technologies are changing rapidly, which is good news for small shops because you'll have the ability to show distant gallery owners, buyers, and customers your work, no matter where in the world you (or they) are located.

▼▼▼

MARKETING MATERIALS

For those who have the resources to produce one, a brochure can also serve as a mini-portfolio of your work. These brochures, known as capabilities brochures, work best when you need to reach hundreds or thousands of potential customers. When you want to get the word out to the masses, a brochure or direct-mail piece will serve as your introduction to your prospective customer.

Putting together a brochure is probably the first marketing action taken by many new businesses. Unfortunately, too many of these brochures fail to deliver because of poor concepts and production values. You offer a highly tactile and visual product and service as a craftsperson. A poorly reproduced photo or line drawing accompanied by specs or amateur copywriting may do more damage than good. An effective brochure can be a powerful tool, but producing a professional-quality one can cost money. If you're considering a brochure, I recommend my comprehensive book, *The Woodworker's Marketing Guide*, which contains a detailed section on producing and using brochures.

▼▼▼

TELLING THE WORLD

Once you've acquired some of the basic tools of marketing, such as business cards, a portfolio and/or a brochure or fact sheet, you need to get them out of your shop and into the hands of your prospective customers. In Chapter 6 we started creating a profile of those customers, including information about where they live and work and how they can be reached. For some woodworkers, customers may number in the hundreds or thousands, for others a half dozen individuals may keep them busy. This information will determine what methods you use to tell your story. Reaching a wide audience means advertising, publicity, mailings and other mass approaches. Reaching a small tightly focused group requires extensive personal contact and interaction to develop the relationships that generate referral business. Either way, you need a strategy and a plan for enacting that strategy. Developing a strategy is the subject of the next chapter.

JOHN DODD:
THE FINE ART OF SELLING YOUR OWN DESIGNS

▼ ▼ ▼

John Dodd is probably what most people would consider a successful "purist" professional woodworker. Working out of a custom shop situated on an idyllic piece of land in New York's scenic Finger Lakes region, John builds high-end art furniture of his own design, selling through galleries and shows all over the country. He also teaches at The School for American Craftsmen at the Rochester Institute of Technology, one of the premier college woodworking programs in the country. Yet, in spite of his apparent success, John remains pragmatic about his chosen skill and profession, offering advice based on 20 years as a pro woodworker.

I asked John what percentage of his work was his own design and his immediate answer was 100%. After years of chasing commissions and tailoring his work to the specific needs of others, John decided that he would make what he wanted and find buyers who had a desire for his work. His ability to make that choice was perhaps 50% psychological and 50% practical: One, his work is at the highest level of craftsmanship and design and his name is recognized in the serious art-and-craft world. In addition, he has found that he can sell his work, something that is not always the case for woodworkers taking the speculative design route.

Early in his career as a furniture-maker, John exhibited in a series of shows sponsored by the American Crafts Council that took place in Rhinebeck, New York, in the early eighties. These were juried shows, which meant that entries were accepted or rejected by a jury. Taking place over a weekend at a local fairgrounds, the shows featured over 500 exhibitors in large tents. Very high attendance meant that his work was seen by an enormous number of individual customers and design and gallery professionals. It proved to be an excellent marketing move, and John developed relationships with several galleries as a result.

Later these shows moved to another location and, as a result, lost some of their cachet and a large part of their attendance. By that point, John was doing quite well selling pieces through a number of galleries and taking commissions in addition to his teaching work. This continued through the eighties, a time generally looked upon as a golden age for

(continued)

woodworkers and other artist/craftspeople. There was a lot of new money floating around and buying art was the rage.

With the recession of the early nineties, making a living as an art furnituremaker became much more difficult. John retrenched and took on commissions for several new "product lines," including decorative screens and multimedia furnishings for corporate meeting rooms. Unlike the conventional product line discussed in this book, John's screens were one-of-a-kind designs custom built for their environments. The concept of the screens defined John's product.

Today John has come full circle and is exhibiting in the large Baltimore Craft Show that takes place in late winter. He has a line of furniture featuring large blocks of old-growth Douglas fir salvaged from old buildings by a local timber-frame company. John selects interesting segments, shapes and finishes them and incorporates them as design elements in stands for objets d'art, benches and other pieces. He makes up a small run of the pieces and offers a few variations to interested buyers. Selling in the four-figure range, his work has done well, going direct to individuals and the trade through shows and galleries.

John and his wife, Laurie, are aware of the forces at work in their market, keeping up with the gallery and art scene through reading, personal contacts and the design professionals they've worked with over the years. Although his work is as close to sculpture as it is to furniture, John does not have an elitist attitude about the business of woodworking. Instead he embraces this part of his profession as thoroughly as he does the craft parts. His advice? Build your own designs, don't offer too many choices, test the waters at the large shows where you can get exposure to huge numbers of people and get as many pieces out in circulation as possible. Once you are in a number of galleries, shops and shows, the checks will come in. And if they don't you must reevaluate your work on every level until they do.

Visiting John and Laurie was a pleasure because they have a very realistic view of what is often seen as an unrealistic way to make a living. They have learned to combine savvy marketing with a personal vision and make it work on many levels. That alone is a worthy goal for any aspiring woodworker.

CHAPTER 9

MARKETING— THE KEY TO SUCCESS

Throughout the first half of this book I've been surreptitiously trying to convert you to the idea of becoming an expert marketer. I take this sly approach because I've found that many new business owners don't understand marketing. This misunderstanding often translates into fear, arrogance or apathy. All the details we've considered have a marketing outlook, whether it is leasing shop space, choosing an attorney or picking an area of expertise. Shop location and size can help you get work. The right attorney can make referrals and recommendations to potential customers. The expert specialty(ies) you choose can help you concentrate on a lucrative target market of customers who require your expertise.

The resistance many of us feel when it comes to selling our crafts often arises from insecurity about our status in the eyes of others. We don't want to push or to be seen as hucksters, or we feel that we're somehow lowering ourselves when we try to drum up business. If you feel any of these reservations about marketing your woodworking, consider this: Who do you respect more, the successful business owner who earns a living by making good-quality work or the hapless craftsperson who blames everyone else for his or her lack of success? We have grown up in an entrepreneurial society that respects hard won success. I hope that you'll agree that one of the great advantages of that society is that people who work hard can succeed, if they work smart at the same time. Learning to market yourself is one of the smartest things you can do for your business.

DEVELOPING A MARKETING ATTITUDE

The keys to successful marketing are not expensive ads, colorful brochures or fast-talking salesmanship. Successful marketing is an attitude that constantly seeks out opportunities to generate profitable work. This marketing attitude is personified by the woodworker who tells the world what he does when he gets the chance, who spots a new place to sell his work wherever he finds himself, who asks for referrals from satisfied customers and who is constantly learning new ways to improve his work and his business. Successful marketing is a new way of looking at the world.

Marketing is your connection with your prospective customers. It is the plan you make for initiating and maintaining the connection; the tactics, such as advertising or direct mail that you use to reinforce the connection; the proactive listening and problem-solving abilities you use to help your customers and the follow-up with those customers that results in referrals and additional sales or work.

For many small woodworking businesses, marketing may consist of one tactic, used regularly, consistently and effectively. For growing businesses, a marketing tactic may be expanded into a coordinated strategy for keeping the connection vibrant. Now we'll look at a simple start-up strategy designed to use word of mouth and referrals to promote your business.

REACHING OUT AND MAKING CONTACT

If people don't know you're around, you're invisible in the marketplace. If they know you but don't realize that you can help them with solutions for their problems, they won't contact you. You must make contact with your prospective customers, whether they are gift buyers, architects, homeowners or passersby at an arts festival. You could simply try to sell your work to unmotivated strangers, or you could use the knowledge you've already accumulated to pick a target audience that wants your work. The latter method makes it much easier to market yourself.

I've chosen the phrase "make contact" for a good reason. You must make the first connection. You might run an ad, send out a brochure, make a phone call or create a compelling display of your work. Each of these actions starts the marketing process. The key word is *action*. In this chapter we're going to create a simple action plan that you can adapt to your woodworking business.

SELLING IS PROBLEM SOLVING

We buy things because we have a problem that requires a solution. The problem may be an inefficient and unattractive kitchen, a gift we need for a friend's wedding or something less tangible. Maybe owning a piece of custom-made furniture will increase our status and, as a result, our self-esteem. Maybe we simply have to get a reception desk built for our new facility before we open or we'll lose business.

Once you've identified your potential customers, you must learn as much as possible about the problems they want you, your skill or your product to solve. You can do this by listening carefully when you meet a customer or someone who can recommend you to a customer. Listen with an open mind and resist the desire to react to what the potential customer says. Just gather information and identify the problem. Once you've recognized the typical concerns of your customers, you can tailor your action plan to address their concerns, one at a time.

A SAMPLE ACTION-MARKETING PLAN

Let's look at an action-marketing plan for Sara's cabinet shop whose bread and butter is custom kitchens. First we'll set some goals. Sara has determined that she needs to gross (cash flow before expenses) about $150,000 to pay her overhead, salaries and earn enough profit to build up her business. Since her average kitchen job is about $20,000, her goal is to get 8 to 10 jobs per year, which will in turn drive her marketing plan.

The customers for her kitchens are upper middle class, well-educated married couples who own older homes in the area's nicer suburbs and up-scale city neighborhoods. They are usually professionals, both adults work and their incomes are in the six-figure range. Fortunately, Sara lives in a prosperous city that has many people of that description. If her area was depressed, her custom-kitchen business would be much less likely to succeed, and she would have to consider moving or developing a product line she could market to other parts of the country.

Sara decides to focus on three neighborhoods with older but gracious homes that are likely to contain many similar residents. She has already done kitchens in those neighborhoods so she has references from satisfied customers and photos of her work. She puts together a simple plan to build her reputation in these neighborhoods. Sara hopes to get two to three jobs from referrals, two to three from a combination of advertising and direct mail and the rest from publicity. She knows that each of these tactics creates synergy when combined with the others, resulting in multiple contacts with her prospective customers.

Her plan suggests the following tactics:

1. Put together an informative brochure telling how the custom design, construction and installation process works from beginning to end. This information-intensive piece will help establish her expertise while offering her customers useful information. A local writer and a graphic designer help her put together the tasteful two-color brochure, and she has 500 printed for a total cost of about $1,000.

2. Print a series of postcards showing full-color photos of kitchens, some detailing and her employees at work in her shop. One will be a before-and-after combination. The back of the cards will have contact information and will offer anyone who calls a free informational brochure on kitchen remodeling (see item 1 above) and a free estimate. She'll have 500 of each (2500 total) printed for a total cost of about $750.

3. Every other month have a local mailing house send out all of one card to a selected list of homes in each neighborhood, chosen by street and zip code. The mailings cost about $250 each for a total of $1,250.

4. Put together a local media list of every publication, talk show, feature editor, business editor and lifestyles editor in her area. Before each postcard mailing, send several copies of the card, a copy of the brochure and a press release to each person on the media list. The press release offers readers and listeners a free informational report on custom-kitchen remodeling if they call her number. Total cost is about $100.

5. Call each of the media contacts three days after sending out the package to answer questions. Because they hear from her every two months, in their minds she becomes the expert on custom kitchens and is often interviewed for lifestyles and special home features. Her postcard photos are often reproduced in the same places.

6. Purchase small display ads in the same publications for a three-month period in early winter and try to get her business profiled by those publications. Three publications for three months costs her $450.

7. Join the neighborhood association, the local builder's group, the Junior Chamber of Commerce and other associations and go to socializing events.

She has dedicated 20 hours per month to these activities, or about one hour every day, usually for telephone calls and customer meetings. Her total annual marketing budget is around $3,750, or about 2.5% of her total sales, a very low percentage. For this budget she reaches 500 homes, five times by mail, several times through ads and several times through articles that feature her business. She also makes many contacts through her participation in neighborhood and business associations, which, when combined with her other marketing efforts, generates a lot of interest.

The results? In this fictional scenario, our shop owner did everything right, spent her money wisely, networked effectively and, perhaps most important, stuck with her plan no matter how busy she was. And my guess is that she was extremely busy. In fact, for her modest goals she may have gotten too many inquiries. This put her in the fortunate position of having choices. She can raise her prices, cut back on some aspect of her marketing or hire more employees and expand her business.

You too can put together a simple plan for reaching your prospects. Whatever your specialty, it is important to remember that making your plan is a learning process. In our example, the custom-kitchen entrepreneur may find that certain neighborhoods, publications or networking opportunities are more effective than others and decide to focus her attention on them. This intelligent response is vital to any successful marketing plan.

As we walked through this example, we touched on many marketing tactics, including advertising, direct mail, public relations and sales. Now let's take a closer look at these and other basic marketing tactics that are used to create a powerful strategy for increasing your profits.

THE TACTICS

Here are the marketing tactics found in the effective marketer's toolbox. In the beginning, it is a good idea to concentrate on as few as two of these tactics, one of which must be sales skills. All of the other tactics are prospecting activities—that is, they are designed to help you contact and meet prospective customers. Once this is accomplished, your sales ability comes into play to make the sale.

Not all of these tactics will work well for your business. Advertising, for instance, is most effective when you choose an advertising media that targets likely customers rather than something, such as a radio campaign, that blankets an area, getting lost in a barrage of ads. Targeting your customers and matching them with your products or services will save you big bucks in your efforts to market yourself. Let's look at the tactics:

Advertising
Whether it is display advertising found in print media (magazines and newspapers) or broadcast ads on radio or TV, advertising is the first thing many new business owners consider when promoting their com-

pany. They are usually shocked when they find out how expensive advertising can be. Here are several ways to get the most out of your advertising dollars:

▶ Target your media and your audience to reach motivated buyers.

▶ Have professionals write and design or produce your ads with a message that addresses the needs and desires of the buyer.

▶ Run the same ads all the time with the same look, tone, feel and message. Consistency is reassuring, suggesting stability and professionalism.

▶ Always run a series of ads over a specified length of time. It takes repeated exposure to the same message before buyers are motivated to take action. It has been estimated that no ad is effective until a reader or viewer has seen it 25 to 30 times. If you can afford only one ad, consider other less-expensive tactics or buy smaller and cheaper ads and run them often.

▶ Consider using display classifieds, cable TV and other inexpensive but widely exposed media. Avoid small publications unless they target your customers specifically.

▶ Negotiate like crazy when buying ads. Rate sheets are starting points only. You'll be amazed at how much you can save by asking for cheap rates, discounts for series of ads and so on. Ask the ad salespeople about editorial coverage of your business if you buy. They will deny any relationship between editorial coverage and advertising purchases, but written articles will be more powerful than any ad you buy.

▶ Be accessible and respond immediately to all queries generated by your ad. Consider getting an 800 number if you advertise out of your local calling area. They are inexpensive and you get billed only for the calls you receive.

Advertising is best for work you sell directly to consumers, such as cabinetry. It is most effective for larger shops that can handle the expense and the number of inquiries it may generate. Leads you don't have time to answer represents lost business and bad word of mouth in your community. Small shops are better off focusing on more personal marketing tactics.

Direct mail

The sample action-marketing plan outlined in this chapter relied heavily on direct mail to tell the world about the company's custom kitchens. It utilized an inexpensive mailer (postcards) with a strong visual component and an offer of free information. Once a request for information was received, the sales process began. Direct mail can be junk mail or useful information, depending on how well you target your recipients. Information about custom kitchens sent to apartment renters is junk mail but sent to the owners of an older home needing an update is useful information.

Central to successful mail solicitation is the list. Pick the right list and you can do very well with very few responses. Even a list of friends and relatives can launch a business. This kind of mailing could be designed to generate referrals by inviting people to an open house at the shop or to stop in and see the new business. Direct mail is a science because you can measure its effectiveness. There are many guides to this powerful marketing tool (see Resources on p. 150).

Telephone

The telephone is a powerful contact tool. You should have a consistent attitude of helpfulness that you always use when talking to prospective or current customers. The phone is also an effective marketing tool. If, for instance, you are seeking work from designers, architects and builders, a campaign of phone calls made to set up appointments to show your portfolio can initiate the personal selling process effectively. When making phone solicitations, your goal should be to obtain a face-to-face appointment. Try not to get brushed off with the "send me your brochure" routine. Go for the meeting where you can do a little selling.

Networking

A lot of people talk about word of mouth being their most effective marketing tactic. What they often fail to realize is that word of mouth is the result of all these other marketing efforts. One of the best ways to generate word of mouth is by networking. Here are hints for successful networking:

▶ Go where the customers are, not where your competitors are. This seems obvious, but too often I've seen disappointed networkers who attended gatherings where they found themselves in a roomful of people trying to sell something. You must try to meet people with an interest in the kind of work you do. For some this may mean attending every gallery opening in town and striking up conversations with gallery owners and collectors. For others it may mean attending a convention of kitchen designers, craft shop owners or independent sales reps. Like the shop owner in our example, you might join local business or community associations.

▶ Don't sell at events, just meet people unless it is a formal networking event such as a business card exchange. Talk to the people you sit next to at presentations, participate in group discussions and ask others about their work. This usually results in a similar question about your business.

▶ Always hand out fresh (not dog-eared) business cards and take theirs in exchange. If you don't have cards, get them now. No one will do business with someone who jots a phone number on a scrap of paper. When you come back to the office with a handful of cards, add them to your file and send out a brochure, information sheet, postcard or note to everyone you met.

▶ Go to events in which you are interested and be prepared to participate. Stay in the middle of the room and join in casual conversation. Everyone usually has an interest in some aspect of your work. Dress the way you expect others to be dressed. You are now a professional and this means looking like one, even if you're at a casual event.

▶ Try to have fun. People are disposed to send business to people they like.

One of the best ways to break the ice when meeting people is to have them recognize your name or your business. The next tactic can make that happen.

Publicity

Publicity or public relations (PR) is often considered a big-company tactic; however it is very effective for new businesses because local media and trade magazines are always looking for angles in their stories. You can almost always get some kind of coverage by sending out a press release announcing your new business if you focus on an interesting story. Unusual specialties, awards, interesting work for newsworthy clients, a new product line and other compelling stories make it easy for an editor to imagine an angle their readers will enjoy.

Publicity also means building a reputation for expertise. If you build Arts-and-Crafts-style furniture, for instance, always put a little historical background about the movement in your announcements about new shows or products. Offer a background sheet that tells how special construction detailing came about or why earlier craftspeople used certain wood and hardware. Stress benefits such as nontoxic, environmentally friendly finishes, unusual features or your company's new policy of avoiding rain forest products. These benefits can generate coverage.

When you get publicity, multiply it by sending out reprints to your past, current and potential customers. Include complimentary articles in your product catalog or portfolio. Send out rotary file cards with your name, business and contact information to editors for their files. You'll get called when they need a craftperson's viewpoint.

Free publicity is seen and remembered better than many ads. Getting free publicity is definitely worth sending out a few press releases and making a few calls. I've seen craft-show exhibitors who sent out a clever press package a few weeks before a show get tons of coverage in the local media as the local news teams scramble to find something interesting for the six o'clock news. You can do the same.

THE PROBLEM-SOLVING
APPROACH TO SALES

These tactics serve to get your foot in the door or generate requests for information or estimates. Next you must do enough selling to make sure that the customers understand what you have to offer. Selling can be best understood if you approach it as problem solving. The customer comes to you because they have a problem you can solve or a need that you can fulfill. Identify the problem, seek out related problems and address all of them and you'll make the sale. Just listen and keep your eyes open for clues. Wait until the customer has finished speaking, then ask questions based on the information you've gathered.

Asking questions rather than giving a speech lets customers sell themselves. It takes the pressure off you, giving you the opportunity to offer valuable solutions. Once you're at the stage where you understand the potential problems, stop. Tell them you'll prepare a quote or show them your product. In the quote or presentation, address each problem and show how your work or product solves it. Finally, listen for additional concerns and try a closing: "If we can work out the [problem, problem, problem] would you be interested?"

Now keep quiet, listen and learn. Any objections such as price, time or scheduling or personal reservations will surface. Deal with the objections and ask for the sale. If you did your homework, you'll get it.

Selling effectively can be learned. There are many useful books and tapes that can help you understand how to do it. Good sales techniques will benefit your customer and can help eliminate low-price competition that doesn't take the time to deal with customers' concerns.

PLANNING YOUR FIRST
YEAR'S MARKETING

Putting together a simple marketing plan in the beginning can make the difference between success and failure in your new business. With a good marketing attitude, you'll start to see the many connections and opportunities that happen regularly. Putting your goals on paper helps you because the action of writing it down gets things moving. Using the checklist on p. 84, write out a simple plan, fill in activities on certain days on your calendar for the coming year and pick a time of day to handle your marketing. Develop these skills the same way you develop your craft and you'll profit from the experience.

MARKETING PLAN CHECKLIST

1. Name of company, contact information, logo and other identity

2. Specific goals for first year (sales figures, quantity, etc.)

3. Description of proposed products, services, salable skills, etc.

4. Description of target customers—who, where, when, how, why

5. Strategy for reaching customers and getting a response

6. Tactics that will be used and what you need to do to create them

7. Calendar of actions you need to take broken down into steps

8. Budget for all actions and calendar for expenditures

9. Sales training and education

10. New product and/or skill development

11. Follow-up plan to maintain contact with all customers

12. Future goals and revision of plan on a six-month basis

Marketing does not have to be mysterious. You can learn to enjoy it. It is important to realize that the success of your marketing plan will be gradual. The actions and decisions you make now may affect your business six months to a year from now. This is why it is vitally important to start your marketing plan in the beginning and stick with it as long as you are in business. Woodworking often causes you to start over from square one after finishing a job. You'll find that you'll only be comfortable when you've got your schedule booked several months in advance, and the only way to accomplish that is to tell the world about your business all the time.

The fact that each job may be your last is nerve-wracking for most business owners. If you make one-of-a-kind items such as custom furniture, planning ahead can be very difficult because you're never sure what your future income will be. Putting together a simple product line that you sell in addition to your custom work can help even out your cash flow and give you a little breathing room between those big jobs. In the next chapter we'll look at how to develop and sell a product line.

PAUL AND BONNIE RUNG:
LLEWELLYN HOUSE FURNITURE

▼ ▼ ▼

I first met Paul and Bonnie Rung at the Cornhill Arts Festival, a large arts-and-crafts festival held in my town every July. I was wandering among the hundreds of artisan's booths looking for woodworking craft items when I came upon a large double-tent display of finely crafted Shaker-style furniture. Unlike most of the craft items being hawked by their fellow exhibitors, the Rungs' work was substantial and priced as good-quality furniture. Intrigued, I introduced myself and we talked about their business and their commitment to the craft circuit as a means of selling their line.

The Rungs' shop, Llewellyn House Furniture, is located outside of Gettysburg, Pennsylvania, in the midst of historic Civil War sites and Pennsylvania Dutch country. While they have a showroom open by appointment, their primary marketing tool is a dozen weekends of travel to craft shows around their section of the Northeast. They fabricate furniture during the winter with several employees and load up their truck and hit the road in summer. They also offer a catalog of their line, which showgoers can take home.

When I asked them about their marketing their surprising answer was that they didn't think they did any! I told them that I thought that the considerable commitment of time and money they invested in the show circuit was the equal of any marketing efforts I'd seen among woodworkers. The Rungs are pursuing a complex marketing strategy, which is comprised of full-time sales; setting up for shows; traveling; arranging entry forms, fees and travel expenses; and preparing a catalog.

Paul told me he was not convinced that the show circuit was working for them in spite of respectable sales. Their line is mainly larger items with larger price tags than most craft-show products, although they make several smaller items such as footstools that can be carried away by buyers. They have a substantial shop with employees and an investment in machine tools, including an automated lathe they use for chair parts. Like many of their contemporaries they are looking for a better way to reach their target market.

That market consists of successful, well-educated professionals who have an interest in the classic Shaker look. Their catalog is illustrated with line drawings that don't convey the quality and finish of their work as well as color photos would. Unfortunately the cost of producing, printing and

(continued)

mailing enough catalogs to generate the sales they need would probably be prohibitive. Paul explained that he was still looking for a good way to reach those well-heeled customers.

We also talked about another part of their business that has proven successful. They offer a woodworker's school with an interesting twist. The enthusiastic amateur woodworker can sign up for a series of classes at their shop. As part of the process they choose and build a piece of furniture to take home at the end of the classes. Paul's staff helps them fabricate the piece using professional skills and tools. He estimated that half the pieces finished in this program were completed with substantial help from his staff and half were largely built by the students under staff supervision.

The result of the school is a win-win situation. Llewellyn House Furniture gets a fee more than equivalent to the sale of the furniture and the student has a one-of-a-kind experience working in a real woodshop, including taking home a piece of furniture as a memento. They are seriously considering going after this unique source of business full time.

One of the interesting things that came out of my conversation with Paul and Bonnie was a new appreciation for the work involved in craft-show sales. Their commitment of resources and time is a big one that is better suited to woodworkers with a line of smaller, lower-priced items than large furniture pieces. Also needed is an outgoing and friendly personality and a high energy level, both apparent in large doses in the owners of Llewellyn House Furniture.

The Rungs have a flexible approach to their craft as evidenced by their innovative school program. They have also sought work turning parts for other shops and have considered going into the kit furniture business. Their ongoing interest in finding new ways to reach their customers is an essential part of successful entrepreneurship. There are many opportunities and options available to the woodworker who keeps an open mind and few to the shop owner who takes a negative approach to marketing.

CHAPTER 10

HOW TO DEVELOP AND SELL A PRODUCT LINE

What to make?

How to make it?

Finding a market for your products

How to price a product

Throughout *Profitable Woodworking*, I've made a point of differentiating between woodworkers who do custom work and those who make a product line. Unlike one-of-a-kind pieces fabricated for one customer, a product line is any item you can make in a production run. This run might be as few as a dozen pieces or many thousands, depending on demand and your shop's capabilities. All of your work may be centered around developing, manufacturing and marketing a line of products, or you may build such an item as a sideline to help with the cash flow.

Even the purist woodworker should consider doing a limited edition of his or her work. Making limited editions enables you to offer your high-quality work to more people at a more competitive price. Not only will this generate cash, it will also place your work with many more customers. In the art world, limited editions of prints, cast sculpture or jewelry are common ways for an artist and/or gallery to improve on income while helping many people who could not otherwise afford to enjoy the more expensive work. You can do the same.

A product line can be simple birdhouses or works of art. In the eighties, renowned woodworker Wendell Castle produced a series of clocks in a limited edition that sold for five figures each. Sold to collectors and galleries, these clocks could, in their way, be considered a product line. Not only did they represent a significant source of income, but they reinforced Castle's reputation as a serious artist/craftsperson of the highest caliber.

A small product offered as a sideline can generate additional sales of your primary craft. In the Jim Plukas interview on p. 96, we find that his line of custom cigar humidors generated over $15,000 in other commissions before he had sold more than a few humidors. Customers interested in his humidors commissioned custom furnishings after they looked through his portfolio while considering a humidor purchase. A production run piece can serve as an introduction to you and your craft.

For many small shops, developing a line of products is their primary business. You see their work regularly, whether it is furniture, wooden parts for other products, cabinetry or picture frames. They sell their work at retail gift shops, through catalogs, direct to manufacturers, at arts-and-crafts festivals and through mail-order ads. Some shops are devoted to mass production and are filled with computer numerically controlled (CNC) machinery that automates repetitive tasks, while other shops may be a solitary craftsperson turning out piece after piece in a basement or garage. Both face many of the same challenges when it comes to choosing, fabricating and marketing a product line.

▼ ▼ ▼

WHAT TO MAKE?

The choices of things to make out of wood are truly staggering. In the commercial world wood is a universal material valued for its beauty, durability and ease of fabrication. It shows up in custom packing cases for expensive instruments, automobile dashboards and many other places. All of these items are made by woodworkers.

Fortunately your choice of a product or products doesn't require you to choose from every possible application of wood. You'll make something based on what you know and on what people will want. A birdwatcher might make bird feeders, carvings or even frames for bird prints. A musician might become an instrument maker or make music stands, stereo component cabinetry, speaker boxes or instrument cases.

The point is that successful products come out of real-life interests and needs. The prototype for a child's desk was probably built for the woodworker's child. A line of compact-disc storage cases might come from an audiophile woodworker's frustration at not being able to find a high-quality storage system for his collection.

Often, a product line comes after you have built a similar item on a custom basis. People see the unique cutting boards, well-crafted bath vanity or desk lamp that you built for a customer and ask for their own version. This is a clear indicator of potential success for a product.

Of course not everything lends itself to multiple reproductions. To qualify for a product line, it must be inexpensive to produce in quantity without sacrificing quality. It must be something that has a wide appeal from a design and finish viewpoint. A custom king-size headboard stained purple may look great in the environment for which it was designed but probably wouldn't transfer well to a showroom or gallery. In considering a potential product line for your shop ask yourself the following questions:

▶ Can I simplify the design without losing its appeal? This can make your product more price competitive.

▶ Are the materials stable, durable and easily worked?

▶ Is the finish simple and can the effect be easily reproduced?

▶ Does the design lend itself to mass production? Pieces with large amounts of handwork such as carving, hand-cut dovetails and other finicky work may be too time-consuming to do in multiples.

▶ Can I price the product to sell profitably after I've considered the markdowns I may have to offer retailers or other middlemen? (More about mark-downs and pricing later in this chapter.)

▶ Does the product require packaging? How much will the packaging cost, and do I need to pay for printing, graphic design and labeling?

▶ Is the product safe, with no dangerous finishes, pieces that can break off, sharp edges, etc.?

▶ Is the product durable enough to be shipped, moved around and handled?

▶ Can the product be easily described and is there a benefit for the buyer?

▶ Do you have a clear idea of who will want the product and how to reach your customer base? (More about your customer base later in this chapter.)

▶ Is it something that interests you? This can be important, unless you are in it strictly for the money. If you have 50 orders for your Victorian House mailbox, you are going to be spending a lot of time putting together mailboxes. Before you commit yourself to any product line, think about the work involved and make sure that it is something your shop can handle and something in which you can maintain an interest.

Once you've chosen a product, done the design and started working on the marketing, you'll get a feel for how well the product is going to sell. It is almost as dangerous to have an overwhelming success as to have a failure. Orders you can't fill can mean anything from angry customers to lawsuits.

When you're jammed up quality may suffer, compounding the problem as you get items returned and deal with dissatisfied customers. It is better to be realistic about what you can handle and limit yourself to that many orders and no more. Consider the first run a test. You'll learn a great deal about your product and all the considerations listed on the previous page. Apply that knowledge and you'll see real profits the second time around.

▼▼▼

HOW TO MAKE IT?

Fabricating a number of identical or similar items requires a different thought process from producing custom work. You must always be looking for ways to use a setup or jig repeatedly. You'll be making many parts and doing many assemblies at once and finishing everything simultaneously.

Mass production often requires different tools from custom work. A tool that may be too expensive or require too much setup time or training to be worth occasional use becomes valuable when you can leverage that price or time by making many cuts, passes or turns. Once you're set up, you leave it that way and crank out the pieces.

Remember the process plan back in Chapter 4? We looked at the way a shop is organized, with dedicated work areas for different tasks. You carry this one step further when making numerous copies of a piece. Instead of going from one work area to another in a cycle, you may set up an area, perform the same task many times then go on to the next area and perform the next step on each piece. This process may mean reorganizing your shop to make more room for multiple items working their way through the process.

Materials and hardware are treated differently too. You'll be buying larger quantities to save money, to ensure a steady supply of material once you are up and running and to get uniform quality. My brother, who makes many cabinets, buys hinges by the case, saving 50% to 60% over local hardware supplier prices for a single pair. He has spent a lot of time looking for dependable, well-priced and reliable sources who will have the stock available in the quantities he needs. He may also build up an inventory of an item when there is a sale or close-out.

Making a product line may require more storage space for supplies and inventory. If you're working with a deadline, making gift items or selling the craft circuit, you'll be building up an inventory for the holidays or the summer selling season. You may be able to rent extra space temporarily from your landlord or use a self-storage unit as a temporary warehouse. You may also need a place to store and dry out wood for future use.

One advantage of the assembly-line approach is that it is relatively easy to hire a helper and teach the person one task at a time rather than teaching a whole craft. Your helper can start producing valuable work much earlier than someone you have to train and teach new tasks every day. You also have the option of subcontracting some of the construction elements of the piece to other shops. You might have someone else handle finishing, multiple operations that require specialized machinery that you can't afford or the sales and marketing of your work. There are many companies that subcontract the entire project and simply focus on the marketing or planning stages. Of course I would question whether they are truly in the woodworking business.

You need to be adaptable in your planning and fabrication. If customers want a particular finish or design that you're not particularly fond of, you'll need to follow their lead, especially since you're making a much larger commitment in time and money compared to custom work.

This brings us to an important consideration when you think about a product line—whether to operate speculatively or only with a firm order or known success in hand. Speculative work is done without prior orders from customers. You create a product, make some and try them out in the marketplace. It is a high-risk situation. You're far better off testing the waters with experienced buyers and only going ahead when those buyers give you a vote of confidence by placing orders and sending deposits.

▼▼▼

FINDING A MARKET FOR YOUR PRODUCTS

There are countless piles of failed products lying around in warehouses, and these products nearly always failed because someone got carried away with an idea but didn't do the necessary homework. As I've stated elsewhere, the market determines your success, and few make it by trying to push something onto the market that it doesn't want or need. For every Pet Rock-type success there are many failures. And remember, Pet Rocks required little or no investment in materials, time or labor!

Design your product after the market tells you there is a need for it. If you have an idea that makes sense to you, try it out on the kind of people who might be potential buyers. Large companies use focus groups to test ideas before they commit to the manufacturing risk. You can do likewise. Build a sample or two and take it around to places that might sell your work. Get professional opinions from people who sell regularly, such as store buyers, other craftspeople at festivals or galleries, or distributors who handle similar items. Consider selling on consignment at a local outlet, and try different prices, colors, designs, etc. Keep your eyes and ears open.

A proven recipe for success (albeit not a particularly original one) is imitation of what you know works. Being the first company on the scene with a new product often means that you do the groundwork (and make the mistakes) for those who follow and imitate. Before you try a totally new idea, ask yourself if you're willing to take the risk of an untested idea. You might be better off making a better mousetrap than something totally new.

Look at successful products and see if you can improve on them or put a new spin on them. Perhaps you can create an accessory item that fulfills a need created by an existing, successful product. Microwave ovens created a huge market for microwave oven carts. Audio and computer compact discs created a whole new storage problem. Computers, kitchen appliances, audio/video systems and a host of new technology items created a whole array of cabinetry requirements. If you can make a better computer desk the world will still beat a path to your door—if they know where it is.

The niftiest product in the world will go nowhere if no one knows it exists. Marketing a product line is different from marketing a one-of-a-kind woodworking product. In your custom shop you might prosper with as few as 10 jobs a year, often getting a number of jobs from the same client. To sell a thousand widgets may require reaching 100,000 widget buyers. Or only one. It depends on your marketing strategy.

To reach the numbers of people required to succeed with a product line you have two choices: Market them yourself or sell them to a middleman who can pitch them to the wider market. In many cases you'll do a little of both. First we'll look at the do-it-yourself method.

Let's imagine you've designed a unique line of cutting boards. You've tested a few of them in stores and at several crafts shows and met with a good response. You may have lost money on your original run of 20 to 30 pieces but you're confident that as your volume increases you'll do well. Deciding to sell them yourself to increase your profit per item, you register for 10 crafts shows all around your area on 10 consecutive weekends in the summer. You buy a display tent and a van and figure that you'll need to sell 100 cutting boards per show to meet your goals. The average show attendance is 15,000 people so it seems reasonable to sell at least that many.

You spend your winter months making 1,200 cutting boards. With a partner, you spend 10 weekends selling cutting boards and sell out. You're a success. Or are you? For each show you have two days of travel and setup expenses for two people and two days of selling, plus accommodations, meals, your display expense, registration fees, gas, vehicle expenses, losses from theft and damage and many small expenses you never expected. If you are lucky you broke even and learned a lot about your market.

You can use that experience for a more successful follow-up year. You'll have better products, get better sites at shows, learn which shows are good and which to avoid, meet experienced, savvy veterans and learn from them and probably have a good time. Or you'll find that you hate it and try something else. Both results are equally valuable.

Let's look at the other approach—letting others market for you. You are an avid cook and you've designed the ultimate cutting board for the serious gourmet cook. It's a premium item and the cooks you've shown it to are knocking on your door, wanting their very own. Because it is an upscale item, you've targeted a catalog company that sells to thousands of serious cooks nationwide. You choose a classy name for your product, develop some sales materials and have some great photos taken by a photographer who specializes in food. You contact the catalog company, send them your information and arrange to fly to their office (at your expense) to meet with them.

You've prepared for the meeting by getting business references from your bank, landlord and attorney, you have photos of your shop and proof that you can deliver on your promises, and you have the financing to put up the capital to make the boards if you get an order.

You have your meeting and they love your boards, they're impressed by your presentation and they'll get back to you. The next meeting goes well but they decline because they already have a source for a similar product. You head home and back to work.

The catalog company calls back and offers you a price for 5,000 cutting boards to be delivered in stages. You dicker a little with the price and, taking a deep breath, go for it. Now all you have to do is get the financing, get the materials, get the tools and get to work. You're a success.

Or are you? It depends—on the price, the terms, the return policy and the response to your product by the catalog's customers. You won't know until you get repeat orders whether you've got a hit. And that could be months down the line.

The point is that you should learn all you can about a product and its market before you make a major commitment to it. I recommend starting out small, possibly doing your products as a sideline to your woodworking business. Pick a niche product and find inexpensive ways to reach those niche buyers. Many successful businesses have started from classified ads and free publicity. A steady stream of orders, even small ones, can do wonders for a shop's cash flow and your state of mind. And if a product is a success, you'll know how to scale up while remaining profitable because you took things slowly and learned the ropes.

HOW TO PRICE A PRODUCT

Product lines are priced differently from one-of-a-kind woodworking projects. Before I walk you through one method, I'd like to take you backward through the price cycle of a product sold in a retail store. Let's look at the height sticks sold by Kids and Colors, Inc. If you walk into a store you'll see a price tag reading: SUGGESTED LIST PRICE $29.95, OUR PRICE $24.95. The second figure is the retail price of the sticks. List price is important because it helps everyone along the distribution chain to set a price. You, as manufacturer, are at the bottom of the food chain, and you must look upward when pricing a product to make sure that your product can handle all the markups necessary to make it profitable on the chain. You may sell the height sticks to John's Toy Wholesaler for $12. John marks them up to $16 and sells them to Jill's Toy Shops, who in turn mark them up to $24.95. It is not uncommon for each stage to involve a 40% to 50% markup.

You can also work backward by offering a discount from list price. If the list price is $30, you'll offer John a discount of 60% ($12), provided he buys in quantity. He, in turn, offers a 53% discount to Jill, who retails the item at about 17% off of list price.

There are other considerations when it comes to selling products to other companies. You'll give breaks for fast payment, quantity purchases, degree of assembly, whether you package them and whether you must take them back at some point (return policy). It's all negotiable.

Once you understand that an item that sells for $25 in a store may only bring in $12 at your end, you'll understand why learning to price your product for your market is so important. You may get an order for 1,000 height sticks and be unable to make any money on them, particularly if you must wait 90 to 180 days for payment.

Fortunately, you have options. It may not be practical to market the height sticks through normal retail channels because there are too many middlemen, all with their hands out. You might do better scaling back and selling them yourself at craft shows, getting the $25 yourself for each sale. Of course you must invest time and money into this kind of marketing strategy. Planning now can help you decide which is the best way for your product. Chapter 13 covers this planning in detail.

So how do you price a product? You're going to have to do it in tiers, based on the quantity you'll be making. You'll need to plan your production line, taking advantage of repetitive processes and setups to turn out many parts for assembly later. This mass production is what makes it possible to sell those height sticks for such a low price. The maker buys materials in quantity, mills and cuts them in batches, assembles and finishes in batches and ends up with a product that costs much less than a one-of-a-kind piece.

To determine your break-even point, you need a formula. Start with materials costs, taking into consideration the discounts you will receive when your orders reach certain volume levels. Add on overhead, which is the figure you derived when you computed your shop rate. For instance, if your shop rate is $30 per hour and you make 40 widgets per 40 hour week, your overhead is $30 per widget. Now add in your profit margin and marketing costs and subtract an allowance for returns or defects. The final number is the minimum price you need to set to remain competitive and profitable.

What if the resulting number is too high or too low? If it's too low, great, you'll make a little more or be a little more competitive. If it's too high, you may need to change your design, make greater quantities, use different materials or try to cut your overhead costs, possibly by having another shop do some of the labor or by hiring an inexpensive assistant.

Pricing is not a matter of picking a number and sticking with it. You have to test prices just as you test a product design. You try things out and gauge the response and adapt accordingly. It can be a major mistake to underprice or overprice a product. Sometimes you may find that a slight reduction in your price will result in many more sales. On the other hand, I've found that small shops can do very well with a high-priced item that retains some of the "custom" aspects of a one-of-a-kind piece. A particular furniture design may prove popular, so you could consider reproducing several at a time and doing some advertising. Many thriving companies have gotten their start with a core product that develops a loyal customer base receptive to other similar items. That is probably the key to creating a successful product line for most small shops.

JIM PLUKAS:
DEVELOPING A PRODUCT LINE ON THE SIDE

▼ ▼ ▼

By developing a line of high-quality cigar humidors, Jim Plukas has found an interesting way to keep himself busy between furniture commissions while adding to his bottom line. As an unexpected side benefit, his humidors have proven to be an effective marketing tool, often generating interest in his general woodworking services. He has received several lucrative commissions from clients who bought humidors from him.

Jim has worked as a professional woodworker for 11 years, starting out after high school. He attended the Leeds Woodworking School in Massachusetts and went on to work with a shop owner he met there. After several years of building high-end furniture for designers in the New York City area, he moved back to his hometown of Rochester, New York, and started his own shop doing similar work.

One of Jim's specialties is veneer work, and many of his pieces feature marquetry and complex pattern matching of exotic veneers. Introduced to the world of fine-cigar aficionados by his brother, Jim realized that he had found an opportunity to combine that veneering skill with a product line catering to a well-heeled market. He developed sample models of three humidor designs, priced from $300 to $1,200, depending on hardware, size and other features. After building several humidors he began taking them to cigar "smokers," parties where cigar lovers socialize in a fragrant smoke-filled restaurant.

Making connections at the smokers led to sales through local cigar stores and a connection with a national mail-order company. Equally important, Jim has made regular contact with an almost ideal group of potential customers for his woodworking business, resulting in commissions for items such as a veneered sideboard, a walk-in humidor for a retail store and several commercial furniture commissions.

While desktop humidor sales have been steady, it is the commissions that have proven the value of adding a product line to his service mix. Jim had his humidors photographed and created postcards and sell sheets that his customers at the smoker functions could take home. These marketing materials were also part of his regular mailings to past, present and future clients.

Jim has found that the most challenging aspect of developing a product line is pricing the product to remain profitable after various middlemen take their share of the retail price. Competition in the humidor market at the national level has been fierce, coming from manufacturers overseas who have the advantages of size and inexpensive labor. After taking a stab at the national market through his exposure with the catalog company, Jim realized that he might be better off selling in his region himself and using the line as an effective introduction to his primary business, James M. Plukas, Custom Furniture & Woodworking.

Jim Plukas's experience in developing a product line is common. Much of the marketing and product development was driven by seat-of-the-pants experience, learning as he went. He got advice from several quarters including various cigar business "experts." The advice varied widely in its usefulness and value. For example, the volume figures he was advised would be likely turned out to be exaggerated, and the price ranges required to be competitive made it hard for the inexpensive models to be profitable. However, the regular sales have added a steady flow of cash to his bottom line, and his commission work has generated profits equivalent to the sales of a lot of humidors.

Jim's advice to those contemplating a product line? Learn everything you can about the buyers, the market and the competition, and pay serious attention to your pricing. When you develop marketing materials, keep them general enough to be useful for a while because printing costs go down considerably when you have larger quantities made. Try to develop a product close to your core competencies and interests so that you can sell those skills for other projects.

BUSINESS SKILLS

In his book, *Growing a Business*, Paul Hawken refers to what he calls "trade sense." Trade sense is an intuitive ability to recognize opportunities and capitalize on them. Hawken feels that trade sense is essential to small-business success. The kid selling lemonade in the front yard, the street performer playing for tips and the successful corporate deal maker share this sense of their market, their customers and the many ways they can increase their profits. I believe trade sense can (and must) be learned if you are going to succeed in your new woodworking business.

Any skill is developed through hands-on practice, and the skills involved in running your business are no exception. Over time, you'll learn how to make the best of unusual situations faced daily by the small-business owner, such as finding reputable suppliers, obtaining financing, problem solving and generating referrals. While some of these business skills will come only from experience, there are many other skills you can learn from books, mentors and teachers and fellow shop owners.

As an entrepreneur you will make choices about minor problems as well as major ones. If you come from a nine-to-five corporate background, you may miss the consensus decision-making process of that environment. It is my guess, however, that you found those processes frustrating or you wouldn't be considering becoming self-employed. The ability to make decisions about your own destiny is both a blessing and the occasional curse of having a self-owned business.

QUALITY

The quality of your work and the way you do business are central to every decision you make, from choosing suppliers to taking a loss to correct a problem. Ultimately, quality will be the major contributing factor to the word of mouth and referrals that are vital to your success. No amount of advertising has the same effect as a great recommendation from a past customer, and no amount of advertising can undo a negative review from that same customer.

It is said that a satisfied customer will tell two to three people about a good experience, while an unsatisfied customer will tell 8 to 10. It's easy to see that you cannot afford to do poor-quality work. You must also strive to guarantee your work and be quick to resolve any problems as soon as a customer brings them to your attention. The decision to offer the highest-quality work and service is one you should commit to now.

Because wood is an organic material, the quality will vary from piece to piece and environment to environment. You're not punching uniform parts out of metal or popping widgets out of molds. Every piece you make must be checked individually for potential problems. Recognizing these problems is an on-going skill you'll develop over the years.

These quality issues require constant education and attention on your part. Many publications are available to help you keep up with problems and solutions offered by fellow woodworkers. Don't just read the hobbyist publications; subscribe to the trade magazines even if they seem aimed at larger companies. You'll find valuable information and many resources in them.

College classes, conferences, trade shows and seminars are very useful as information- and skill-building resources. Your local professional tool suppliers probably offer seminars. In between the sales pitches you'll find a lot of information that can both save and make you money—and you'll meet your fellow woodworkers.

You may have noticed that I haven't discussed competition. That's because I believe that fellow woodworkers should be considered valuable resources. After all, they know more about your business than anyone else because they are in the trenches just like you. Because of the increase in specialization, you'll seldom find a fellow woodworker making exactly what you make. And when you do, quality and your level of business skills will often put you ahead. This is especially true in head-to-head bidding, where your reputation and sales skills can help you beat a lower bid.

COST EFFICIENCY

Back in the sixties, big business embraced a group of consultants known as efficiency experts. These engineers did time-management studies on every imaginable work process, looking for ways to shave time, increase productivity and cut corners. They eventually disappeared because their mechanical approach to human labor alienated the workers whose jobs their studies affected. As a result of such studies, "efficiency" has a dehumanizing ring to it.

However, pursuing a craft is also a process of finding the most efficient ways to work. Many woodworking books can show you how to streamline your craft and take advantage of your skills. In your business you'll need to focus as closely on your money-saving skills as you do on your woodworking skills.

Cost efficiency is important for several reasons: cost savings, increased profitability and competitive prices. You may also find ways to avoid repetitive tasks while profiting from their efficiency by buying some pieces instead of fabricating them.

Cost efficiency doesn't always mean getting the cheapest price. Buying cheap materials often means excessive waste, quality problems, problems with finishes and an inferior product. Getting the best materials can mean more money and fewer hassles.

You work in an environment that is very detail oriented when you are a craftsperson. Often this detail orientation includes hardware items, for example. Why would anyone fabricate a beautiful dovetailed box only to save a few cents by using cheap hinges and clasps? Instead of taking this penny-wise, pound-foolish approach, look for ways to buy in quantity. You'll find that buying high-quality components in quantity from professional suppliers will cost less than buying in limited numbers at cheap hardware-store prices. The trade magazines listed in Resources (see p. 150) are a good place to start.

Labor is a primary place to consider cost efficiency, and again the wages you pay may determine the quality you get. Often a few extra dollars an hour may mean getting a skilled worker who accomplishes more work with less supervision and fewer problems. An unskilled but cheap worker will demand a lot of your attention and time, which means you are paying the equivalent of both your wages combined, with less work accomplished!

TIME AND QUALITY OF LIFE

Woodworkers often have the feeling that they start over in business with each new project. Only by acquiring skill and powerful resources can you increase your profits while improving the quality of your life. This "life-quality" thinking can determine your use of the limited time you have. For instance, as a cabinetmaker, you may be considering the use of precut and drilled 32mm cabinet parts from a factory as an alternative to buying plywood and doing the work yourself. It is relatively easy to weigh the advantages and disadvantages monetarily. You compare material costs, labor costs and time spent, and you may find that it is much cheaper to buy a sink base than to make one. You may also realize that moving sheets of laminate ply around your shop all day is not the most interesting way to make a living. Instead you may decide to focus on the more interesting woodworking aspects of the job, such as fabricating doors and drawers.

These decisions are rooted in your preferences for how you spend your time. Some woodworkers only feel comfortable making everything themselves, even if they make a very low hourly wage. That's their choice. However, I urge to you to take some time to consider the gains and losses inherent in your choices. When you analyze your profits, both material and psychological, you may be surprised by the results. You may find that a decision to outsource some of your work can have a far-reaching impact on the quality of your life, giving you additional time and energy for doing more interesting work or simply having more personal time.

OUTSOURCING FOR PROFIT

If time is money, then having others do some of your work for you can be an easy way to save both. Outsourcing means finding outside resources that you can use to do some of your work for you. This procedure has the potential to increase your profits and free up your time for the activities you do best. In the cabinetmaking example above, outsourcing means taking advantage of a factory shop's mass-production tools and methods to save yourself money. The 32mm cabinet factory buys plywood in volume and uses CNC-automated machinery to produce high-quality cabinet panels quickly and cheaply. You may find that such a shop can supply you with boxes that are virtually identical to those you fabricate yourself but at a cost lower than you could ever match. Consider the cost of plywood, your time, shop tools being tied up and the drudgery of drilling several hundred shelf holes. Compare such activities to the ease with which you could call in an order that fits your requirements exactly, specifying a finish or surface option and receiving precut and edge-banded cabinet boxes a few weeks later. The prices in this outsourcing example are low enough that you can charge for your time in specifying and assembling the cabinets and mark them up for an excellent profit. In the meantime you're focusing on using your best skills.

Outsourcing can mean hiring another shop to perform certain steps of a job. Such steps might include veneering, applying special finishes, metalwork, multiple-parts fabrication or any other stage of your work that requires specialized tools and/or expertise. The important considerations are quality and profitability. If you can ensure both, you should seriously consider outsourcing.

It is not unusual for a part-time woodworking business to concentrate on design, prototyping and marketing and to outsource the actual fabrication. While this may seem a far step from the craft end of woodworking, it can be a formula for success when you're running the show. It can also provide a way to try out a new product or business concept without making a significant investment in tools, shop and labor.

Developing extensive resources for supplies is another requirement for success. Every piece of hardware, unusual cabinet insert, lighting component or other added part is an opportunity to make additional profits from a job. Developing resources also allows you to offer a complete service, which may give you an advantage over a competitor who can't handle the extras.

Professional suppliers cater to pros in the field, not to the hobbyist crowd. You are now a business and may deal with suppliers who sell to wholesale buyers. Prices will be lower and you can take advantage of quantity discounts. This means that you get the markup that is normally passed on to the consumer and it builds a profit margin into every job.

▼▼▼

YOUR SHOP AS A RESOURCE

Outsourcing can come your way from others and be a significant source of business for you. If you specialize in woodturning, for instance, and own an automated lathe, you could offer your services to other shops requiring limited runs of turned items for a reasonable price. Becoming a resource for others can bring you more income, and thus greater profit. If you have specialized skills, consider assembling a simple flyer to send to other shop owners offering your skills.

WORKING WITH SUPPLIERS

You'll need to develop business relationships with materials suppliers in your area. You can get help from other woodworkers and contractors to find these resources. Provide your tax ID number, business cards and brochure, if you have one, and request accounts with the suppliers you'll be using regularly. They'll want credit references from your bank and anyone else you already have accounts with and may require you to buy on a cash basis for the first few months to prove you are legitimate.

Once you have accounts, use them and pay promptly. This establishes your business credit and may help you get loans in the future. This is important because getting loans for home mortgages and other purposes can be difficult when you are self-employed. Having an account also means that you become a valued customer. You'll learn about upcoming deals and seminars, get speedy service, and the suppliers may refer work to you.

Try to plan ahead and buy in quantity to receive a discount and avoid costly last-minute trips to get supplies. Commonly used materials such as screws and sandpaper should be bought in bulk. Shopping around, particularly with mail-order suppliers, can save you a lot of money.

THINKING GLOBAL

With the advent of rapid delivery services like Federal Express, you no longer have to wait weeks for mail-order shipments. This is a major benefit for small shops because you can have access to large suppliers with complete inventories who may be located on the other side of the country. They may offer lower prices because they buy in quantity and their overhead is low because they've often chosen locations that are out of the way. These savings are passed on to you, meaning greater profit and lower inventory cost.

Finding suppliers is easier if you go through the trade magazines and request catalogs from anyone who carries products you may use. Build up a resource library and check the quality of their services by placing a few small orders. If they are always back-ordered or lacking in expertise or service, try someone else. You'll eventually develop a network of global suppliers that will enable you to say, "Sure, I can get that."

Specialized suppliers of items such as finishing materials or veneers often offer useful information about new products in their catalogs. They may be able to give advice over the phone, and some offer weekend seminars where you can learn new techniques and skills. Utilizing expert resources can mean having help available in a crisis, when you really need it, and the help is often free. As you develop relationships with these full-service companies, you may find their advice as valuable as their products.

▼▼▼

ON-LINE RESOURCES

If you have a computer and a modem, access to a wide variety of woodworking and business resources is only a few mouse clicks away. With the explosion of the Internet's business area, the World Wide Web and easy access via the major on-line services such as America Online, Compuserve, Prodigy and others, you have access to incredible resources and customers all over the globe. It seems that a new information source for woodworkers comes on-line every day. These range from e-mail discussions about specific subjects to specialized home pages filled with information about tools, techniques and almost any aspect of your craft.

Once you're on-line you'll find these sources through easy-to-use directories supplied by the service provider. And once you've found a few sources, you'll be led to others. This kind of access is one of the biggest benefits of the on-line world. For small businesses, the Internet offers an even better benefit—access to motivated customers all over the world.

Electronic mail, or e-mail, is a basic benefit of subscription to any on-line service. With it you gain an instantaneous and very inexpensive method of communicating with your clients. In many cases you can send documents over e-mail making possible an interactive design process among you and clients such as architects or designers. If you've chosen a niche business, the Internet makes it very easy to find people with a specific interest in your area of specialization.

As an example, you may specialize in audio/video home-theater cabinetry. There are many forums on the net that cater to audio enthusiasts and professionals. By cruising these areas and listening in, you'll find contacts who may be interested in your services. Simply e-mail them and talk about your work. Or hook up with a related page on the Web and offer your services. You can include photos, text and contact information.

Eventually, you may put your portfolio or product line on the Web for instant and easy access by anyone considering your services. Very soon using an on-line service will be a normal way of reaching your customers. We will also be seeing virtual catalogs and ordering from suppliers who will be able to fill an order directly off your computer.

These on-line business services are available to anyone for a very low monthly fee. It's worthwhile to have an e-mail address. You'll be surprised how many of your current customers will jump at the chance to communicate via e-mail. Eventually the novelty will wear off, but right now e-mail's simplicity, speed and low cost have made it an accepted way of communicating globally. There's no reason why you can't join in.

▼▼▼

KEEPING THE CUSTOMER SATISFIED

It's said that the customer is always right, even when he or she is wrong. There will be times when you'll have to cope with nightmare customers, inconsiderate customers, cheap customers, lying customers and every other kind of customer. However, once you agree to do business with troublesome customers, you must still try to satisfy them until the job is finished. The secret is to learn how to identify and avoid these people before you commit.

It's hard to say no to work, especially when things are slow. If you take a job you have second thoughts about, try to have a plan for coping with potentially bad situations. Get as much money up front as possible. In the agreement, spell out exactly what you will do and when, and get it signed. Include a method for dealing with change orders and extra work, and spell out when the job is officially complete. You can specify an hourly rate for extra work. Use your shop rate. Often, knowing that they will be billed a substantial hourly rate for extras will stop some customers from taking advantage of you.

Once you commit to providing a service or delivering a product, you must do everything possible to keep the customer satisfied. One of the most effective tactics for handling this is to think in terms of getting the job finished. Have a target date, track your progress in writing with the customer, and as you near completion put together a "punchlist" of tasks that must be completed to reach the end. You and the customer can use the punchlist to make sure you are both in agreement about what constitutes a finished job and what constitutes extra, billable work.

Deadlines are essential in woodworking as elsewhere. Some of you may resist the idea; however, I've found that most woodworkers come to value a firm deadline because it gives them a wrap-up date beyond which they can expect payment. Deadlines also help you plan a series of projects to avoid having too many things going on at once.

To the customer, a deadline may be vital. Someone purchasing a product or custom piece may have plans for giving it as a gift or may need it to meet a business deadline. You must deliver on time or you'll face an angry and unhappy customer. In some cases you may also be fined for lateness, particularly on commercial construction jobs. Meet with your clients and work out a schedule in writing as part of your agreement. Always try to beat your deadline and build in a little cushion for potential problems.

If you have problems with a project, keep the customer informed and be honest about what is happening. The earlier you let the customer know there may be problems, the more likely it is that they'll be willing to work with you. Don't procrastinate in telling them about problems, and try to avoid making a string of excuses. As a professional you are expected to anticipate problems and have a backup plan. When a supplier gets back-ordered or something needs to be redone, tell your customer and cooperate with him or her to find an alternative solution.

The reason for your dedication to service is twofold: You have sold yourself as a solution not a problem, and you want to generate future business and referrals from your customers. Part of the quality and service you provide is follow-up after the sale, and the benefit you gain is more business.

▼▼▼

REFERRALS

Once you get rolling with your wood shop, a large percentage of your business will come from referrals and past customers. Satisfied customers are your number-one source of future work. They create the word of mouth that brings in business. They make recommendations to friends and business associates. They serve as a reference you can cite to potential new customers. Your association with them confers respectability and credence to the claims you make in your marketing.

I recommend that you compile a checklist to maintain contact with past customers. This checklist could include some of the following steps:

1. Put together a customer list on your computer. Keep track of work you've done, referrals your customers have made, important dates, such as birthdays, and up-to-date contact information.

2. Schedule an informal contact program for every past customer. Holiday cards, newsletters, copies of articles you've written, a new stack of brochures or business cards and other mailings can keep these customers aware of your existence and any new services or products you offer so they'll continue to feel involved in your success.

3. Call past customers every two months to check on how they're doing and to touch base. An informal call may remind them of a project they're considering or keep you in mind when they hear of potential work. Keep it short and friendly.

4. Ask for referrals. This is critical. If you ask your customers to keep you in mind when they hear of someone who needs the services you provide, they will recommend you. People like to make referrals because it makes them look well connected while providing a valued service to their acquaintances.

5. Treat referrals with extra care. Your past customers put their reputations in your hands when they make a referral.

6. Reward those "key" people who make regular referrals. Buy them lunch. Send them gifts you've made. If you see an article or book they will be interested in, buy it and send it over with your compliments. These thoughtful gestures can generate significant amounts of business.

7. Make referrals yourself. Send business to your customers. If your lawyer gets you business, try to recommend him or her.

Once your network of past and current customers is working for you by referring customers to you, you'll probably find that much of your business comes from these contacts. A referral from a respected source is better than any advertising. Combine it with effective marketing and you'll stay busy and profitable.

There are many tips and tricks of the trade that can help you develop trade sense. I've included a few and I know you'll develop many yourself as your experience grows. Stay open to new ideas. Read business and self-help books for insights. Subscribe to magazines that cater to entrepreneurs like you. Talk to other woodworkers and small-business owners and share experiences. Ask for referrals from your suppliers, the professionals who help your business and family and friends.

Doing business is a skill and an art. You learn by doing and observing. Treat it as a challenging game and you'll prosper on many levels, from monetary to the quality of your work life.

RICHARD EDIC:
A CABINETMAKER GOES TO OUTSIDE SOURCING

▼ ▼ ▼

There are several routes into professional woodworking, of which one of the most common is the woodworker who started out as a carpenter. Often, woodworkers with carpentry backgrounds tend to do more cabinetry and permanently installed work as opposed to free-standing furnishings. Their installation and carpentry skills give them an edge over the furnituremaker, who tends to focus on joinery and detailing, only to be confronted with the inconsistencies of the real world during an installation.

Richard Edic (yes, he's my brother) began working as a carpenter, soon focused on finish carpentry and then opened a woodshop with a partner. For several years they handled everything from furniture commissions to sculpture fabrication and engineered-wood projects. After his partner moved away, Richard found himself concentrating on the cabinetry end of the business, designing and building high-quality kitchens and commercial cabinetry.

Early in his cabinetmaking career, Richard embraced the 32mm system, also known as European-style cabinets, which feature standard hardware and shelf support systems and are further distinguished from conventional cabinetry by the lack of a face frame on the cabinet cases. Special hinging systems and overlay doors eliminate the need for face frames, simplifying construction and offering a sleek, contemporary look.

The 32mm system was developed specifically for manufacture by modern computer numerically controlled (CNC) machines in a plant or large shop. These machines typically use computer-controlled routers and drilling setups to turn sheets of laminate and veneer plywood into uniform, high-quality cabinet parts. These can be shipped knocked down and assembled on site using a standard glue-and-dowel system in predrilled holes. The cabinetmaker adds custom doors, tops and hardware and has a finished product.

At first Richard was building his own cabinet cases, moving sheets of plywood into his shop and drilling the seemingly endless numbers of holes required by modern cabinetry one at a time. Because the cost of CNC machinery is beyond the range of most small shops, it wasn't practical to invest in the technology. As a result, he was limited in the number of jobs he could take on. Then he discovered he could buy outsourced cabinet parts, literally transforming the nature of his cabinet business.

Now he purchases the majority of his cabinet boxes from a CNC-equipped factory in Colorado. Once the kitchen is designed, he faxes his cabinet requirements to the manufacturer and gets back a quote. After the order is in, Richard will go to work building doors, counters, trim and any specialized cabinetry the job requires. A few weeks later the cabinet parts arrive knocked down on a skid, ready for assembly. All parts are included, even glue. He mounts the hinge plates with Euro screws that fit any hole in the cabinet system, assembles the cases and mounts the doors. Often this fabrication may take place on a job site, making it much easier to deliver a large number of cabinets. With a helper, the cabinetry for a large kitchen can be assembled in a few days.

The biggest criticism many cabinetmakers have of outsourcing is that they are losing work. Richard's experience has shown that outsourcing actually improves his profitability and the quality of his workday. Instead of hauling heavy sheets of plywood around the shop and performing endless numbers of repetitive tasks, he gets an inexpensive high-quality product, which allows him to focus on the creative end and add the custom treatments that make each project unique.

From a cash-flow standpoint, outsourcing has meant generating profits from marking up other people's work. It also means that he can compete with the home-center cabinet companies and offer a higher-quality product. Even more important, outsourcing has meant that Richard can focus on the design and installation of the work, guaranteeing client satisfaction while getting more work done with less time and effort.

Richard's marketing strategy is based primarily on word of mouth reinforced by several marketing tactics. He had a good-quality four-page, two-color brochure done by a top local graphic designer. He sends these out to anyone who requests information and as a follow-up piece to referrals. His past clients get a pile to pass along to friends. He has also done mailings to a list of local architects and designers, resulting in commissions for a wide range of commercial and residential work.

Richard says that outsourcing saved him as a professional woodworker by making it possible for him to stay competitive in a business dominated by large cabinet companies. He feels that his edge has always been design and the ability to integrate his work into a larger picture, whether it is a client's lifestyle or a complex construction schedule on a commercial project. Ultimately he feels that 90% of his work will always come from referrals, and satisfied customers are the source of those referrals. Outsourcing has helped him create a great product that keeps the work coming in.

WOODWORKING SKILLS FROM A BUSINESS POINT OF VIEW

The place where your woodworking and business skills merge is the point where you become a professional. A professional knows that the primary restriction he or she has on profits is time. The professional woodworker is always looking for more effective ways to utilize this valuable, but limited, resource.

As your skills in the shop improve, you will be able to do a better and faster job. This translates into more income, higher-quality work and satisfied customers. In this chapter we're going to take a look at the shop skills you have from a business perspective. You need to start thinking about new ways to utilize your skills, new skills you may wish to learn and when it makes sense to hire others for their specialized abilities.

▼ ▼ ▼

THE VALUE OF YOUR TIME

In Chapter 7 when you computed your shop rate you were doing an exercise in time management. If your shop rate is $30 per hour, you can tell approximately what your time is worth. A 10-minute phone call took $5 of your time on the job. A day off is worth $240. When you figured to spend 10 hours doing a job that took you 8, you increased the value of your time by $7.50 an hour.

Manipulating numbers like this is interesting for several reasons: You can tell how you are doing, where you can improve and what activities, skills or tools made you the most money or provided the most satisfaction. As your experience grows, you'll start to recognize your strengths and weaknesses. You'll know what skills to emphasize and what jobs to pass on to others or avoid. Knowing the value of your time gives you a basis for making decisions, even if you lack the hands-on experience.

Your shop rate is only one basis for evaluating your time. When you learn a new skill or teach an assistant a new skill, your time is worth more than your shop rate because that skill needs to be learned only once and can then be used over and over again. Skill building is an investment that saves you time in the future and doesn't differ from making an investment in a tool or in shop space.

The value of your time can help you make decisions by helping you set priorities. When you are juggling several jobs at once or facing multiple deadlines, setting priorities is a must. Let's look at one effective way of setting priorities and making decisions.

It's Wednesday morning and you have several choices you must make regarding the rest of the week. You are building a reception desk for the corporate headquarters of a retail-store chain. They need to have it installed Friday afternoon because their CEO is coming in on Saturday. You need to make a pair of custom-designed bookends as a gift for a wedding you are invited to on Saturday. A new customer calls after getting your name out of the phone book and wants to know if you can repair his antique table if he brings it in today. Finally, it's a beautiful day and a friend calls to try to talk you into taking the afternoon off to play golf.

Where do you place your priorities? You won't be happy if you show up without a wedding gift on Saturday, the retailer could be a significant source of future business, but you'll have to work your tail off to complete the reception desk for this new deadline, and that new customer is the first call you've had as a result of your new ad in the phone book. His small job would pay to run that ad for several months. Finally, it's a beautiful fall day and the golf course beckons.

The way out of this dilemma is relatively simple. Whichever action will benefit *you* the most becomes your number-one priority. You could apply this criteria to the others and create an order of importance. But wait a minute. *The action that benefits* me *the most?* I can understand if you're confused. If you think about it, the action that benefits you the most is seldom the one you might enjoy the most. Playing golf would be the easy choice, but in our example it is probably the least beneficial, unless you're totally stressed out and really need a change.

I cannot tell you or our imaginary woodworker which action is the most important to him or her. That's why the benefit is chosen by the recipient. You might choose the reception desk because it will mean more work, a big check and a job finished. You may decide to put aside a few hours in the evenings to build those bookends. And you may tell the call-in customer that you're tied up till Tuesday but you'll be happy to see him then. Finally you make an appointment to reward yourself with a golf game on Sunday, weather permitting.

We have all experienced the conflict of too many demands on our time. The only solution to this situation is to set priorities according to your best interests and take the first step your decision-making process calls for. The act of writing down your to-do or action list, putting it in order (prioritizing) and choosing a first step is vital.

One of the essential tools for running any business is a planner. Get one that can be updated, has places for notes and addresses and use it all the time. Keep it on your desk, on your truck seat and near the phone at home. Instead of jotting things down on wall calendars, Post-its, pieces of paper and the backs of business cards, put everything in your planner. Keep your family and social obligations in there along with your work appointments. That way you'll never double schedule, forget an important event or not have a phone number handy when you're away from the office.

Recognizing the value of your time is one of the most powerful skills you'll ever acquire. It will help you avoid long meetings, side trips and wasting time on busy work. Remember how much each minute is worth and tell your clients you have another appointment, send an assistant on those errands, put the busy work on the back burner and take care of the priorities. The remaining tasks will find their way into your schedule when they are important enough.

The more effective you can be with your time management and skill building the more your time will be worth to others.

▼ ▼ ▼

SETTING UP A SPECIALTY SHOP

When you specialize in one type of woodworking, you can command more money. Why? Because your expertise means you'll get the job completed faster, better and with fewer hassles.

Specializing does not necessarily mean giving up other aspects of woodworking. You can play both sides, develop several specialties or stick to one thing only. If you become an expert at working with veneers, for instance, you may find that your skills can translate into working with other surfacing materials such as laminates, specialized metal surfacing or unusual pattern matching of solid woods.

Specialties often develop as you find yourself handling certain problems repeatedly. You may have a specialty and not recognize it. The following skills evaluation can help you recognize marketable specialties. Many a sideline business has come from an expert who began instructing other enthusiasts, supplying hard-to-find parts or offering a specialized service to other hobbyists. You can do the same by selling your specialty as a service to other woodworkers, both professional and amateur.

▼▼▼

SKILLS EVALUATION

The marketing attitude we discussed in Chapter 9 is particularly valuable for selling your specialized skills. Once you've discovered a few areas where you excel, think about the possible uses for those skills and who would pay to make use of them. To begin your evaluation, take a look at the skills you use regularly.

List the different skills you currently have. Skills are abilities learned through study and hands-on experience. You cannot learn skills from books. You can learn valuable information that saves you time and experimentation, tap into the experience of others and learn about processes from books, but you must actually perform the operation to acquire skill at it. If you've read everything published about hand-cut dovetails but never cut one, you are not an expert. If you've cut hundreds in the course of your work, you have a valuable skill. Some skill areas include:

- finishing

- lathe work, woodturning

- carving

- cabinetry

- veneer and marquetry

- laminating and bending

- joinery

- estimating, quoting and sales

- design work

- drawing, photography, CAD work (computer-aided design)

- installations

- product development

- short-run manufacturing

- specialized tool ownership and use (CNC drilling for instance)

These skills can be marketed as services or specialties. They have many subcategories. For instance, specialized tool ownership and use might include tools you own that other shops are unlikely to purchase but may have an occasional need for. Automated lathes, CNC tools, large planers, shapers and other high-tech or exceptionally powerful tools can earn their keep and yours if you offer your services to others as a subcontractor.

Almost any specialty can become more profitable. Artist woodworkers often have very specific niches. They might focus on unusual one-of-a-kind boxes. Within that category they may make only complex puzzle boxes or conceptual works of art. Once the specialty is chosen, creative minds will see the possibilities, even as they may feel they are restricting themselves. Having a creative approach will help you find ways to capitalize on your special skills.

▼▼▼

SELLING TO OTHER CRAFTSPERSONS

You're working in your shop and a local interior designer calls, wanting to know if you can supply him with 120 stair spindles for a historic restoration his firm is working on. Because you have faithfully read this book, you instantly reply, "Let me call you back with a price," and finish the phone call with a thank-you. You take a look at your lathe gathering sawdust in the corner and wonder if you and it can handle the job. Then you remember that Joe down the hall has an automated lathe he uses for table legs in his line of Shaker furniture. You call him and ask him if he can supply you with the legs, giving him the particulars. He says sure and calls you back with a price. You call the designer and quote him your price which includes a nice markup for you. He says great and sends out a check.

Two weeks later Joe calls you and asks if you do veneering. You tell him yes, in fact you specialize in it and have a new veneer press. The next thing you know you have an order from Joe for the veneer work on several tabletops. He tells Gary at the lumber yard that you're a specialist in veneers, and Gary sends two customers to you for veneer work.

When you sell your work to other shops, you can be price competitive because you have no marketing costs, fewer and shorter meetings and don't have to deal with parts of the job for which you are less qualified. Earning this kind of money can be easy, particularly as your skills develop and you acquire specialized equipment and the knowledge of how to use it.

SUBCONTRACTING WORK TO OTHERS

The other side of this story is the value of subcontracting some of your work to others. Instead of turning down that spindle order, you were able to fill it, make a profit and keep a valued client happy, with very little effort on your part. You didn't incur the expense of the lathe and the time and materials required to complete the job. You took some risk by trusting Joe, but you'd worked with him before and respected his reputation. And he returned the favor by sending work to you.

Very few shops actively utilize the skills of their competitors or try to sell their skills. Some simple marketing, perhaps a fact sheet and a call, can generate work for you from your fellow shop owners. At the same time you can add their specialties to your list of profitable resources. The same goes for craftspeople from other disciplines. I know woodworkers who use jewelers to cast custom-made decorative hardware, glass shops to provide special glazing and metalworkers to fabricate custom metalwork. All of these artisans and businesses are potential sources of business for you.

TIME ANALYSIS

In the section on estimating in Chapter 7, you broke the job down into stages and estimated how long it would take you to complete each level. What do you do when you can't estimate how long you'll take because you've never done something before? When you gain more experience you'll have a better idea of how long such jobs take to complete. Until then, you need to think about a time analysis of your working methods. I'm not talking about a scientific study. You simply need to do a little analysis of your work each time you complete a job or task. How long did it take? Where did you run into trouble and how would you do it next time? How much extra time do you need to budget to cover those trouble spots? Asking yourself these questions regularly will accelerate the learning process and help you when you prepare estimates in the future.

If you're having trouble estimating a complex or unfamiliar job, ask questions of other woodworkers, suppliers and your customer. Break the job into smaller steps until it looks familiar, then start your time estimate.

Developing an ongoing sense of your abilities and how well you manage time is truly a business skill. You'll get it in the long run by trial and error or much faster by using the analytical tools you have and the experience and guidance of others.

KEEPING THINGS TOGETHER

Are you having fun yet? This brief chapter is dedicated to those of you who may be a little overwhelmed by everything you must consider when starting your woodworking business. After all, the idea was to get into something you really enjoy and make a decent living from it, right? Yet, after reading this far, it may seem that we've talked about almost everything except woodworking. Lawyers, money, marketing, sales, outsourcing—things that may not have been on your mind when you first considered woodworking as a business career. Now it seems that I'm asking you to spend far more of your time dealing with these issues than with those that may really interest you.

It is very difficult for new business owners to understand the many hats they are expected to wear regularly, rain or shine. Unlike an executive with a large organization, you don't have a dedicated support staff and a roster of experts available to deal with these demands. That's why one of the major focuses of this book is about finding ways to work with others who are in similar businesses. Not only can they provide that working support, they also help you cope with many of the things that can overwhelm a small business. In a sense, they become your co-workers.

I've also focused on money a great deal, forever looking at ways to increase profits and cash flow. This is because there is nothing more demoralizing than stacks of bills and no work to generate the money to pay them. Fortunately, you are in a business that can be turned around pretty quickly with a few marketing activities. The money is there to keep you from experiencing the stress that many small-business owners suffer from. Learn these skills now and you'll be happier.

Trying to learn so much new information can cause a mental overload at first. Gradually, you'll absorb and organize your new knowledge subconsciously, and things that were abstract will suddenly become clear. Understanding usually comes when you find yourself in a real situation, learning and using the skills covered in this book. Only when you take action does this happen. Planning your actions then making them happen have a way of clearing your mind. Things that may be confusing or overwhelming at the beginning become commonplace and normal later on. You can prevail by simply planning a little in advance and then taking the leap of faith to go on.

▼▼▼

DO YOU HAVE A LONG-TERM PLAN?

We've looked at many things you must consider when starting your new shop. One is something you might call "the six-month wall." This is similar to the "wall" that marathon runners often hit when they near the 20-mile mark. Because many of the actions and complications of starting a business keep you busy for the first six months or so, you become so involved in what you are doing that you stop looking forward and focus entirely on the tasks at hand.

Focusing on the present is fine, up to a point. But when your day-to-day work takes over and you stop performing actions that will pay off for you in the future, you have hit a wall. These actions include marketing, planning new projects or products, looking for new sources and suppliers and developing relationships that generate referrals. Often when you hit this wall, things seem to be out of control and you start to feel that no matter how hard you work you can't catch up or get ahead.

Inevitably, this occurs because you don't have long-term plans, you need to update your plan or you've stopped following the plans you've made. Your actions seem to be movement for its own sake rather than progress.

This may not happen to you, but if it does, you may need to update your plans and extend them further into the future. Planning is an organic process that evolves as circumstances and experience change. Your original plan may not work anymore or you may have discovered an interesting side road that headed you in a new, more promising direction. It's time to plan for the long term.

PLAN TO ACT: THE BASICS OF PLANNING AND GOALS

There is a saying: "Watch what you ask for because you just might get it." This not only means to be careful, it also means once you've made plans they take on their own momentum and things happen. For example, a woodworker decides to build a chair, starting with a sketch and refining the sketch into a final drawing. He then uses the drawing to make a materials list, decides on a construction plan, and then proceeds until the chair is finished and ready to go to its user.

By the time the chair is on its way out of the shop, the woodworker is thinking about better ways to fabricate it, variations to the design, the chair's potential as a gallery piece or something that can be produced in quantity, or how he lost money making it and what he'd do differently next time. That kind of thinking is what creates long-term planning.

Every few months, you should sit down with someone who understands your business and go over your goals for the next couple of years. Name some specific goals you'd like to accomplish and include some fantasies you'd love to have happen. Anything goes because this kind of brainstorming helps you learn what really interests you, even if it seems unreal at the present. Just write down your goals and study them.

There are a few things you should consider when setting goals:

▶ They should be your own. Other people's goals are fine for them but you must formulate goals that are attractive to you.

▶ You should be able to imagine the first step necessary to put your goals into motion. If you have no idea how to accomplish a goal, you need more information. Your goal should be to acquire the knowledge you need.

▶ Assign specific timelines and values to your goals. Don't say, "I want to make more money next year." Say, "I am going to make $45,000 net by December 199-." Specific goals start you thinking about specific ways to accomplish them, and deadlines help you stay motivated.

▶ State your goals in a positive voice. Recent studies indicate that our brains may be incapable of accurately processing negative commands. Listen to this statement: "Don't think about the color blue." You couldn't not think about blue without first thinking of blue, could you? Positive statements work better because they eliminate one step in the mental process. Life is tough enough without getting entangled in negative thinking.

▶ Put your goals in writing and share them with someone else. If possible, make it a combined effort, with each of you helping the other. Writing down your goals is the first action that gets you started.

▶ For each goal, note the steps you must take to achieve that goal. The actions should be simple enough to be accomplished easily. Read a book, make a call, buy a tool, learn a new trick of the trade, give everyone you see in the next week a business card—these goals are easy to accomplish and they offer gratification and encouragement, which take you to the next action.

▶ Give your goals three dimensions. One of the most effective motivational tools used by great leaders is to create a compelling and realistic destination. If having your own commercial shop space is your goal, visualize the space, furnish it with the tools and materials you'll need, smell the sawdust and feel the floor under your feet. Try on this imaginary shop for size, play around with your options and use the inner model you make to help you get started on achieving your goal.

Plan a monthly goals discussion with your associate, a mentor from a school or small-business office, or a friend. Update and adapt your plans as your conditions and interests change. The planning process can be very exciting when you realize it means that you have some control over your destiny as a business owner.

▼▼▼

LEARNING AND TEACHING

In business as in life, change is the only constant. Your business and your woodworking skills must adapt to changes in your market, people's tastes, new competition and many other unpredictable events. Sometimes the old way may not be the best way. Just as no one works with bronze hand tools or water-powered take-off machinery, you may need to adapt and learn to use new skills and resources. Computers, 3-D design, water-based finishes and 32mm cabinet systems were all new a few years ago and have now become standards. Those who fail to learn and adapt may be left behind.

Keep up to speed with the latest tools and techniques by reading the trade and enthusiast magazines, attending shows and seminars, and taking classes in both woodworking and business skills. A basic marketing class at a local college will give you valuable insights on building your business and will also offer excellent networking opportunities. Your instructors can often become mentors or sources of business referrals.

Teaching what you know can also be lucrative and educational. Most high schools, community colleges and adult education programs are on the lookout for instructors. You can teach a class or two in your specialty and meet potential customers and workers and establish yourself as a recognized expert. Look for opportunities to tell the world about the craft that is so important to you. Many organizations are in constant need of speakers, and woodworking is a subject that interests many people. It's not only good business, but it's an excellent way to discover some of your own strengths and build self-esteem.

One of the prices that self-employed people pay is a lot of time spent in solitude, working on their craft and business. It's important to consider your psychological state as well as the state of your shop or business. Find fellow business owners and share your experiences. Maybe you can put together a biweekly breakfast group of business owners or communicate on-line via the Internet with many other woodworkers and small-business people out there. You'll find that it is easy to get others to join in because you share many of the same daily challenges.

It is vital to look forward and inward as you build your business. It keeps your work interesting, it attracts customers and it helps you develop the strength and confidence to succeed without too much stress. After all, it is supposed to be the great American dream to own your own business. Why not enjoy it?

CHAPTER 14

GALLERIES AND THE ART WORLD

The art of woodworking may sometimes seem to get lost as we look at the business of woodworking. Yet even woodworkers who consider themselves first and foremost as artisans must deal with the world of commerce if they want to prosper. Selling work that springs entirely from your imagination is as great a challenge as selling a line of toys or a cabinetry job. You must find motivated buyers or benefactors who can help support your artistic quest.

While woodworkers will sell some works directly to individuals, most of their sales and publicity will come about as a result of gallery representation. Galleries provide the all-important high-profile exposure woodworkers need to survive and thrive. Galleries are showrooms, with a clientele that has a serious interest in your kind of work, a network of related galleries and art-world contacts and the know-how to build your reputation. In exchange, they receive a healthy percentage of the sales price, from 40% to 60% or higher.

If this seems exorbitant, you must consider the rarefied world with which you are dealing. One-of-a-kind furnishings, sculpture and artwork are not for everyone. The price is often too high for the average buyer, and galleries may or may not be interested in your work. Galleries are run by people, and people make decisions based on many factors, such as personal taste, aversion to risk, and many other intangibles. The person who is interested in fine-art furniture and other woodworking is more likely to follow certain artists through the galleries who represent them.

The subject of marketing art is touchy for most artists. Your gallery representative can take on responsibility for marketing tasks you may have no desire to handle. In this chapter we're going to look at ways you can start to build a reputation as a woodworker and get gallery representation.

▼▼▼

THE FINE-ARTS WOODWORKER

What exactly is "fine-arts woodworking" or "art furniture," two terms often used to describe the art-world version of woodworking? For our purposes, I'll define them as being the creation of items for their intrinsic aesthetic appeal entirely by or under an individual's supervision. While that is quite a mouthful, it covers several important considerations. The work is appealing because it is original. Because some complex or large pieces may be fabricated in parts or entirely by others under the designer's supervision, my definition is not restricted to the artist/craftsperson who does everything alone.

One man's bread is another man's poison, as the saying goes, and when it comes to art this is particularly true. You may conceive and build a chair that one person loves and another loathes without your ever intending either reaction. Because of this individuality, your marketing is wholly aimed at finding the former—that person who has the means and desire to support your art.

In the discussion that follows, I'm going to concentrate on art furniture-makers rather than sculptors or conceptual artists who work in wood. Most readers are likely to be furnituremakers, particularly as they start out. Even if you are a sculptor, I believe you'll find the information useful.

▼▼▼

ART FURNITURE: CREATING ONE-OF-A-KIND PIECES

Functional art furniture is more likely to get you into a gallery than nonfunctional, conceptual work. There are many galleries that specialize in artist/craftspersons and, more particularly, woodworkers. The route artist/woodworkers have taken is defined by the decision to make their own work without outside interference. To fit my definition, their work must be unique in design, superlative in materials and workmanship, and aesthetically appealing.

For the artist/woodworker to sell to a gallery, it's necessary to have a track record and body of work to show in a portfolio, a willingness to meet and greet the people who can move your career forward and the ability to deliver your work as promised. It's also important to learn your way around the art world by educating yourself through reading, attending shows and events, and meeting people who can serve as mentors and actively participating in your own career. It requires considerable personal energy, like any other calling. Because your portfolio is so vital, I'll begin with a look at your body of work and how to assemble a portfolio.

ASSEMBLING A PORTFOLIO

A portfolio is more than a collection of prints or slides of your woodworking. It should show your body of work. A body of work demonstrates dedication, continuity of vision, growth and the development of your craft. A portfolio filled with a random selection of projects without a thread of artistic vision will probably not land you gallery support. The portfolio that displays a body of work with a commonality to it will get attention.

Beginners are often caught in a double bind. They haven't done enough original work to make an impressive portfolio, and they cannot get the commissions to develop the body of work without them. If you have only recently begun working as an artist/woodworker and your gallery portfolio is limited, you have some work to do. Because you'll need to design and fabricate a number of pieces on spec (without a firm commitment from a buyer, from the word *speculation*), you'll probably need to use some of the techniques and advice in the rest of this book to get work to pay the bills.

The time, money and energy you put into your body of work is a part of your education and development as a woodworker. If you stick to it you'll receive a return on your investment for the rest of your life. I recommend having 6 to 10 major pieces in your portfolio before approaching the galleries. This work should have a common vision that represents your current artistic achievement. Unless they are exceptional, pieces from your past should probably be omitted, including school projects, work crafted at a level below your current abilities, outmoded designs and other dated pieces.

Limiting your past work means doing new design and fabrication work over several months with the specific goal of creating a knockout portfolio that is current and cutting edge. The advantage of planning your whole portfolio and executing it all at once is that you can have your pieces photographed at the same time, and you can demonstrate the development of your craft, which will help you make a powerful presentation.

TAKING THE BEST PHOTOGRAPHS

Always photograph all of your work. Whenever possible, and especially for portfolio shots, use a professional photographer with experience shooting arts and crafts. He or she usually has a studio, large-format cameras, lighting gear and a great deal of experience in making your work have that special glow to make the image really pop. Find these photographers by asking other artists, gallery owners and by checking out their portfolios. You'll spend money but it's worthwhile, particularly if you have a number of pieces shot at the same time. You may be able to work out a trade or a volume discount. It doesn't hurt to ask.

I don't recommend shooting your work yourself, but if you must, check out the detailed section on photography in *The Woodworker's Marketing Guide* listed in Resources (see p. 150).

You'll want both color negatives and slides of each piece because galleries and shows will often accept submissions only in slide form. Once you meet face to face with a gallery rep, a print portfolio is essential. Shoot a variety of angles, emphasize details with lighting, clean and polish the work thoroughly and shoot a lot of film, capturing details, interiors of casework, special hardware or finishes, etc. If you do not have a lot of work in your portfolio, these detail shots can beef up what you have. For the full-piece shots, consider putting a vase of flowers or some other nondescript decorative object in to establish scale.

PUTTING IT ALL TOGETHER

How important is your portfolio? Until you are established as a well-known artisan, your portfolio is your showroom, sales tool, biography and first contact with the art world. It is important and deserves some thought when you put it together.

You don't need to buy an extremely expensive leather portfolio case when you're starting out. Instead spend your money on high-quality printing and darkroom work done by a professional lab. I recommend getting a minimum of 10 copies of each print. If this is too costly, get three copies and make another 10 high-quality color photocopies. (These will be used to assemble 10 portfolios to mail to gallery owners.) Have copies made of several slides of each piece and put them in clear archival-quality sleeves that can be stored in a binder.

Organize your portfolio as a presentation to illustrate your design process, the construction details of your work and the concepts you follow as an artist. You might practice showing the portfolio to a friend who has not seen your work, trying out various methods of organization, starting and ending with your strongest work. These practice runs help you see your work from a distance. If the person you're showing it to has an art background, so much the better. Listen to the friend's comments and suggestions and make changes to boost your book's impact.

Often you will not be present when your portfolio is reviewed by a potential contact. Put together a one-page table of contents, giving brief descriptions of each piece, any unusual history or construction and design notes and the current owner if he or she is known in the art world (ask first about dropping anyone's name). This table of contents with a brief letter of introduction and your business card will make up the first two pages of your portfolio.

Earlier I suggested making 10 copies of each photo. I've found that an exceptionally effective marketing technique for fine furnituremakers is to put together 10 or more inexpensive portfolios and send them directly to gallery owners, designers or any other significant person who can promote and sell your work. While this may seem expensive, it has to pay off only once to justify itself. You can purchase inexpensive black plastic portfolio binders with clear sleeves for around $5 each. Add the cost of 10 color copies at $1.50 each ($15) and a mailer envelope with a prepaid return label, and your cost per portfolio is about $25 each. (Check with your shipper, since most offer prepaid return labels. The recipient simply puts the portfolio back in the envelope, reseals it and hands it to the shipper.)

FINDING A GALLERY

If you live in a large metropolitan area, finding a gallery may be relatively easy. If you're in the hinterlands or even in a midsize city, finding the right gallery will mean going out of your locality. Fortunately, many crafts galleries don't care where you live if you and your work are salable.

Galleries that feature woodworking are unlikely to work with painters and other studio artists. The galleries that feature a mishmash of styles are not your best bet because they are unlikely to attract patrons with a particular interest in crafts, as opposed to fine art. Your best bet is to start with galleries that have a reputation for handling furniture. You'll find these galleries advertising in the arts-and-crafts magazines listed in Resources (see p. 150). I highly recommend subscribing to several of these magazines and reading them to learn about trends, the interests of specific galleries and buyers and, most important, to get names of individuals associated with these galleries.

The goal of your research is to get the names and contact information for 10 to 12 galleries, whether you get them from fellow woodworkers, magazines and other reading, teachers, professors or the grapevine. Once you've assembled your list, call the gallery for the name of the person to whom you should direct your portfolio.

You can concentrate on galleries and dealers in your geographical part of the country or cover the country as a whole. Shipping and communication are so efficient today that I don't see any advantage in limiting yourself to one section of the country. Once you have representation, the gallery will want an exclusive agreement for your area. Until then, put out a net for the best prospects.

What will you be sending out? Your package should include a personalized cover letter, a brief bio, any reviews or positive press coverage and your portfolio, if you've put one together. Alternatively, you can send sheets of slides or a few photos. Keep everything simple and let your work speak for itself. Say that you are seeking gallery representation and that you'll be calling to get some feedback.

I've found that asking for expert advice and input often generates a friendlier reception than a simple plea for representation. When you call, and you *must* call, ask if anyone has had a chance to look over your work and say that you'd like some input. Be quiet and listen because you can get a lot of information you would have a hard time finding elsewhere. If possible, try to set up a meeting at your shop or the gallery to show your work in person.

I think that follow-up is as important as making the initial effort. One inexpensive tactic is to send out a color postcard of a piece every two months to all of your galleries, clients, media contacts, and so forth, to build and maintain your profile as a viable artist working in wood.

ENTERING SHOWS

You are going to be asked about two things when you approach a new gallery: publicity and what shows you've exhibited in. Thematic or regional shows are often the first step to becoming one of a gallery's stable of artists. Your marketing efforts will probably result in invitations to enter seasonal shows with other craftspeople, shows based on themes such as

"Art Furniture of the Nineties" and group shows of artists associated with a gallery. Besides invitational shows, you will find open entries announced in publications, by arts organizations (join, join, join) and by local galleries. Wherever possible, enter your work. If you are accepted, start your publicity campaign so that when reviewers and art critics attend the show, they'll be looking for your work.

After you've been in a few shows, you'll have more to put on your resumé. Eventually your work will get reviewed and you can put together a sheet of press clippings. Your ability to get press coverage of your work will influence gallery owners because publicity is their most effective marketing tool. Publicity helps generate the word of mouth that sells art.

GETTING GOOD PRESS

Getting publicity for your work is not as difficult as it first appears because the editors of most media have a never-ending need for interesting stories and good photos that will appeal to their readers. Give them local names and an engaging angle and you'll get coverage. By local names I don't simply mean your geographical community. Different disciplines have their own kind of communities, including several in which you, perhaps unwittingly, may be a member. Such communities might include woodworkers, the art world, the fine-crafts world, furniture designers, tool users, small-business people, artisans in general and many other niche groups, each with their own methods of communication. Go to your local library and compile a media list from the library's resources. Target your press releases and information to each of your communities, drop your name and the names of other community members and have an angle that grabs interest.

The angle could be a one-sentence description of the story: *Local Woodworker Wins Best of Show at Quimby Gallery,* or *Unique Computer Furniture Showcases Unusual Designer's Talent*. Once you have an angle you can write a press release, send it to your media list and follow up with a call to the editor or writer handling your interest area. The sample press release on page 129 shows a simple formula for a standard press release. If you can't write it yourself, get a writer friend to help you. In any case, remember to keep it simple and don't leave out any necessary information, such as dates, places, names and so forth.

Publicity is not hard to get if you're creative and write a straightforward, interesting release. Many times publications will print a press release word for word, a good reason to get it right and imitate the style of the media.

YOUR OWN SHOW

The ultimate goal of working with galleries (aside from sales) is the one-person show. Unless your work is extremely compelling you probably won't get a solo show for a while. You typically work your way up, doing group shows, exhibiting one or two pieces, then doing a show with two or three other artists, then a solo show.

The time to go after a solo show is when you have a body of work that represents a significant achievement or new level of commitment on your part. Planning for such a show can start years in advance because of the time required to design, build, plan and publicize these important events. When you get to this point, your gallery representative will be well on the way to making you a known and successful artisan.

EXPANDING YOUR REPUTATION

The next step is a big one. It means moving up to the level of a nationally recognized figure in the art world. Only a few of the many artists around have the talent or desire to go this route. You may do very well as a regional artist or as a recognized specialist in a particular kind of fine-arts woodworking such as woodturning or chair making. In either case, the decision to expand your horizons will probably be made by the collectors and buyers who support your work. They vote with their dollars and their interest to determine who reaches the top. All you can do is your best.

FOR IMMEDIATE RELEASE

Date: September 12, 1995
Contact: Max Gert (777-777-7777)

Local Artist Revives Grandmother Clocks as Functional Sculpture

Woodworker and artisan Max Gert will show his series of Next-Generation Grandmother Clocks at a gala reception in The Atrium Gallery on Saturday, October 1, 1995. The six mantel-size clocks feature unique aniline-dye finishes and jewelry-quality metal ornamentation. The clock style is based on the Arts and Crafts movement while incorporating modernist design elements. A limited edition of 10 sets are being made to order.

"In designing and fabricating this set, I sought to revive the idea of a studio as design atelier," says Gert. "My partner, Chris Zyslinski, and I hope to see our shop, Arcadia Woodworks, develop a reputation as a center of fine woodworking craft and design. This series was conceived as the first products of our fine-arts studio. We still continue to do business as a high-quality woodshop and feel that this kind of work is an excellent complement to that part of our business."

The clocks feature hidden doors, mechanical works and fit well with a contemporary interior. The grandmother clock is smaller than the grandfather clocks we are familiar with. The smaller scale allowed the artist to build a series that is both functional and beautiful.

The show at The Atrium Gallery starts with an opening reception on Saturday evening at 7 p.m. The show will continue through November 15 and is open to the public. For more information, call Marcia Smith at The Atrium Gallery (777-666-6666) or Max Gert or Chris Zyslinski at Arcadia Woodworks (777-777-7777). The Atrium Gallery is located at 495 Main St.

SAMANTHA STEIN:
FOUND MATERIALS AND A DIFFERENT PERSPECTIVE

▼ ▼ ▼

Talk to any woodworker with 20 years of experience and you'll often find someone who has tried many routes to find a center as a craftsperson. Samantha (Sam) Stein is no exception. She dates her first interest in woodworking from seeing Wendell Castle lecture in St. Louis during a cross-country trip in 1976. As a student at the Maryland Art Institute, Sam found Castle's work inspiring enough to decide to take up the craft. Over the past 20 years she has worked in a wooden toy factory, a furniture collaborative, as a corporate furnituremaker, as a restorer of a museum collection and, most recently, as an artist who chooses wood as her medium.

Sam's work owes as much to sculpture as it does to classic woodworking. She works exclusively with found materials and marvels at the quality and quantity of material available to anyone who takes the time to scrounge through woodlots, construction sites and anywhere that brush cutting or natural disaster has left trees down. Often the materials dictate the work, and her interest in the natural shape and texture of limbs and vines predates the recent craze for twig-and-vine furniture. Although her pieces appear regularly in galleries and shows with no particular bias toward woodworking, she makes regular sales.

While Sam has worked as a full-time woodworker for many years, she is currently involved with an artist-in-residence program in a local school district, where she and other local artists and craftspeople work with the students. Her program is similar to those found in many communities and offers an opportunity for artists to earn a stipend for their work with the students. She recommends calling the school districts in your community and asking about similar programs.

I was interested in Sam's experience as a woman working in what has traditionally been a male-dominated field, particularly because of the variety of her experience. She quickly responded by telling me stories of being tested over and over again by her male coworkers in spite of her extensive experience. And despite the prejudice she faced, she remains enthusiastic about woodworking and woodworkers, chalking up her experience to what she laughingly refers to as an "incredible" amount of insecurity on the part of her male coworkers.

At this point in her life, being a woman no longer has a negative impact on her work and may actually be a marketing advantage. Her work doesn't reflect what she sees as a tendency on many woodworkers' parts to focus on the craft rather than the design. Her art background and self-confidence may have led her into design areas not normally covered by her male counterparts. As a result, her work not only sells but generates a lot of interest and commissions.

Sam works in a small garage during the summer hiatus from school. Her tool choices are minimal and include a drill press, a band saw and a full complement of hand tools. She works with chain saws, grinders and chip-carving tools, and her pieces feature a lot of hand work, including joinery and carving. She often incorporates carved pieces such as the life-size brown trout that serve as back slats on a recently made chair. Because her materials are found objects, they include odd building materials, recycled wood from other projects and a wide assortment of oddities such as hollow logs found in a city dump, fallen trees and cut-offs from other shops. Combined with a high level of craftsmanship, the results are unique pieces with a distinctly non-"woodworkerly" look.

She plans on returning to work as a full-time shop owner when her two daughters are older and less dependent. However, she says she will not go back to building contract furniture and conference tables, preferring to carve out her own niche as an artist with a unique vision and wood as her primary material.

Sam's advice to others includes using one's unique skills as an advantage when marketing oneself. In her case, she had a strong portfolio and drawing skills developed in art school. These got her through the door and into the galleries and shows where potential buyers can see her work and contact her for commissions. She firmly believes you should stick to your own vision and stay open to the materials and opportunities around you.

THE NONTRADITIONAL WOODWORKER

The traditional image of a woodworker is the furnituremaker working in a small shop making high-quality one-of-a-kind pieces. In reality, these custom woodworkers are only a small segment of the larger world of wood applications. You may have come to woodworking from a background in engineering, design, art, carpentry or a seemingly unrelated discipline such as teaching or a factory production job. The transition from these occupations may seem difficult until you educate yourself and see how woodworking connects with other kinds of employment.

One of the most effective tactics you can learn when starting out is to look for ways to use your previous experience. Perhaps you had an office job where you worked on the phone and with a computer. You may have insight into a better computer desk, some need that companies such as your former employer might have that is wood related or an idea for a product that appeals to office workers. Your idea could be a gift item, a desk accessory or a component for another office item. Those of you with engineering backgrounds may have an interest in design work, engineered wood or an idea that is a patentable invention.

In this chapter and the next we'll look at some nontraditional ways to make a living as a woodworker. The information in these chapters may help you spot opportunities you overlooked.

OTHER THINGS MADE OF WOOD

Wood is used as a component in many items, from modular office furniture to automobile dashboards. For example, I do a lot of work as a consultant with recording studios. Besides being found in the large amount of cabinetry they use, wood is part of the expensive recording consoles, as the material in computer-designed sound-control surfaces for walls and ceilings, in the desks used by producers and editors, as custom speaker cabinets and in many other places.

Specialized use is often so unique that it is not cost efficient for a large manufacturer to set up a woodshop in an electronics factory to fabricate a few custom parts. They subcontract the work, and there is no reason why a small shop like yours cannot go after the business. By keeping your eyes open for nontraditional uses of wood, you may find untapped market opportunities.

PROTECTING YOUR DESIGNS

Another idea that can lead to substantial financial rewards is inventing new products made of wood and new products used by and for other woodworkers and woodworking businesses. As any woodworker knows, the mail-order tool catalogs are packed with gizmos for woodworkers. And woodworkers are constantly designing new work or inventing new ways to do things. Sometimes those designs can be turned into profitable inventions and products.

Inventors are among the largest targets for con artists, in part because an inventor is often an optimist, ready to believe that the world is as excited about their new idea. This makes inventors ripe for unscrupulous operations that prey on people who dream of striking it rich with some invention. Beware of companies selling expensive packages of information for inventors that have no real value.

If you have an idea or invention that you think may be valuable, you'll need to educate yourself about how to protect and promote that idea. While it is beyond the scope of this book to cover such a large subject, the following is a quick overview of how the idea/invention process works. There are books listed in Resources (see p. 150) that go into much more detail, and I recommend you read them before you put time and energy into an invention.

PROTECTION AND IDEAS

Let's say you have an idea for a new tool or jig or a design for a unique piece of furniture. Before you start counting your money, be forewarned that ideas alone are not always protectable and are seldom original or profitable. To see a profit from your ideas, you must be able to "reduce the idea to practice,"—in other words make a working model—and you must be able to protect the idea with a patent or patents and/or other legal protections.

What makes an idea great? If what you make is something that inspires people to buy it immediately, you have a winning idea. A coffee table with a CD player in it may be unique but I doubt it will create a need in enough consumers to be a worthwhile invention. Only research and testing would tell. On the other hand, a tool that instantly simplifies a repetitive task performed in many manufacturing processes might very well be of great value in such operations because its value can be proven.

Once you have an idea, build a working prototype, which is much more valuable than a drawing or description. You can demonstrate it, try it out, determine how expensive or difficult it is to make and use, refine it and use it to reinforce your claims of originality. Once you have a good working prototype, you can start thinking about protecting your idea.

Ideas are protected by having as many unique aspects about them as you can develop. Unusual engineering, physical appearance, a great product name that can be trademarked, packaging and other unique identifiers can help you prove you were the first to develop the idea. The more of these elements you can add to your original concept, the more likely you are to have a protectable idea.

Patents come in two forms. The patent most of us are familiar with protects a new product or idea that has unique features and can be reduced to a working model or prototype. A design patent covers a unique design, for something like a chair or furniture item, but is limited since it only protects the exact physical design. You should consider a patent only on a product with great commercial potential because it is both expensive and time consuming to get one. Unless your claims in the patent are rock solid and highly original, you are still subject to rip-offs and challenges that can be costly to defend.

If you have an idea that you think is worth a patent, go to a patent attorney before you get too far into it and get a professional opinion. Patent attorneys are specialists, so your regular attorney won't be any help.

If you decide to go after patent protection and your patent attorney agrees, he will prepare the patent application and hire a search firm to research existing patents to determine whether your claims are original. Once the research is done, the application is sent in and you wait for a decision. All of this costs money, and the total can run into thousands of dollars. On top of that, there is no guarantee that you'll get a patent. Then, having a patent is only the start. You have to defend it, find a way to make money from it—either through a licensing agreement or manufacturing and marketing it yourself—and constantly improve it.

It is my opinion that you should consider building and marketing your new product without a patent. Instead use trademarks and the advantages of being first in the marketplace to protect yourself. Get legal advice but don't write off your idea just because of the cost of patent protection.

▼▼▼

WORKING WITH OTHER TRADES AND DESIGNERS

Inventions are one aspect of nontraditional woodworking. A far more common one is to offer your shop's services to other businesses as a resource for wood components, prototypes and custom pieces built to other designer's plans. Connect with other companies such as tool-and-die makers, small manufacturers, metalworking shops, office-furniture dealers, interior designers, architects and others who create and design items with wood components. Ask to bid on any woodwork they need. You may have to price making hundreds or thousands of a small item but this kind of work can pay the bills for a small shop.

Often these companies do not have a regular working relationship with a woodshop or need additional resources to stay competitive. Simply mailing a flyer describing your abilities and a follow-up phone call can generate requests for bids.

PROTOTYPE BUILDING

A specialized example of this kind of woodworking, and one that utilizes all of your skills, is furniture and product prototyping. Manufacturers of wood products often go to outside craftspeople to create original versions of a new product. These prototypes are used for planning, setting up production machinery or marketing a product to a company's customer before manufacturing. Building them requires knowledge of wood manufacturing techniques and materials, along with an inventor's mindset about problem solving and streamlining a design to make it easier and cheaper to make and sell.

If you have experience in these areas or have an engineering background you may be able to break into prototype building by contacting manufacturing companies. Don't limit yourself to your geographic area unless you're in an area with a high concentration of wood-related businesses. The best way to meet potential clients for this kind of work is at major machinery trade shows and through ads and articles in the woodworking industry trade magazines listed in Resources (see p. 150). Many of these trade magazines are free and offer yearbooks that list suppliers and woodworking companies, such as the *Wood and Wood Products Red Book*.

ENGINEERED WOOD

Engineered wood is a new area of some interest to the professional woodshop owner. Engineered wood is loosely described as wood-material products that are designed and manufactured for stability and ease of use. They include various particle boards, medium-density fiberboard (MDF), laminated beams and structural wood products, fingerjointed moldings and other nontraditional wood-related materials.

Developing expert knowledge and skills working with these materials can also generate shop business. They enable you to offer reliable solutions for various problems, they're cost effective and they often have a lower environmental impact—a major consideration in many projects.

All of these areas represent the more commercial aspects of the woodworking craft. As your business grows and your sphere of influence widens you may find similar opportunities. The decision to go after these nontraditional sources of income will be based on your own needs and interests. A good way to succeed in your new business is to keep your options open and consider other potentially lucrative sources of income.

In the next chapter we'll continue this discussion by looking at what I call profit centers—sidelines you can pursue to build your business, improve cash flow or try out a new aspect of your craft. In Chapter 10 we looked at the nuts and bolts of developing a product line as a profit center. Now we'll look at other potential sources of work for your shop, sources that can mean the difference between mere survival and real prosperity.

PROFIT CENTERS

Profit centers are business areas you develop to improve your bottom line. They may begin as sidelines and develop into your primary business or they may remain small parts of your work that you continue to pursue because they make money and/or are an enjoyable diversion from your normal shop routine. As in the last chapter, my purpose in writing about profit centers is to encourage you to stay open-minded about what you do and how you can profit from your abilities.

If you are successful at your primary business you may have no need to think about other sources of income. However, developing profit centers can help you identify future business sectors, give you an opportunity to pursue different skills and protect you from the "too-many-eggs-in-one-basket" syndrome that can put highly specialized businesses at risk. Besides being profitable, profit centers help continue your education both as a woodworker and business owner.

▼▼▼

EXTRA MONEY MAKERS

Creating a profit center is a little like moonlighting in your own business. If you are a general woodworker, a profit center offers a route into developing a lucrative specialty while keeping your current customers. If you specialize now, profit centers offer a route into another specialty that diversifies your customer base and income sources. This diversification, if not carried too far, is an excellent way to manage risk.

One important consideration in creating profit centers is to stay focused. Try to avoid dipping into too many areas or starting too many projects. A profit center is like a minibusiness within your primary business. Its advantage is that you can utilize the structure, knowledge and resources you've already accumulated. In other words, once you have the business set up, the shop equipped and your skills developed, why not use them in new ways?

Often, a profit center comes into your work life as a one-time project. You are asked to write an article, build a gizmo, teach a continuing-education course or design a kitchen. One thing leads to another until one day you realize that you have a sideline and you enjoy it. We're going to look at a few of the many potential profit centers you might pursue in this chapter. Before we do let's consider what makes a good choice.

Your profit center should fit the following general guidelines:

▶ It should be an extension of an existing skill, interest or product. If you build kitchen cabinets and a gift-shop owner asks you to carve 25 bird bookends, you'd be violating this guideline unless you have established some skill at carving birds. Stick to what you know as a starting point.

▶ You can get started on a small scale without a major capital expenditure. Deciding to open your own gallery shop is akin to starting a whole new business that requires new skills and a large infusion of money and labor. Joining an existing cooperative gallery shop with several other craftspeople may offer a better entry into the retail business.

▶ The profit center does not substantially interfere with your existing business. Writing articles about woodworking or teaching a class can usually be done as a sideline during the evening or when you are not in the shop.

▶ The profit center should be profitable, at some point. That's why I call them profit centers. If they don't generate income, they are hobbies.

▶ The profit center should connect to your primary business. An example is the product line that serves as an introduction to a shop's custom-woodworking abilities.

▶ The profit center should have expansion capabilities. Can you spin off related products to existing customers? Can your articles become books? Can you use your teaching experience to generate publicity for your shop or perhaps start an in-shop school?

These criteria can help you avoid gearing up for a project with a limited range that ends up wasting your time and detracting from your primary business. Stick to what you know and seek out customers whose special interests coincide with your own. Let's look at a few potential profit centers that could be adapted to most woodworkers' interests.

PROJECT PLANS FOR SALE

If you ever pick up a woodworking magazine aimed at hobbyists, project plans are popular items—as articles in the magazines and as products sold by various publishers and individuals. If you have an interesting or unique design that can be adapted to the hobbyist market, you may be able to sell your plans.

Because these plans are not designed for professional shops, they often feature dimensioned lumber, simple joinery, hand-applied finishes, readily available hardware and construction that does not require special tools or setups. The market for plans that fit these criteria is limited only by your imagination. Pick up any special-interest magazine and you'll see opportunities for plans. Garden furniture, cooking utensils, sporting equipment, boat accessories, birdhouses, computer desks and dozens of other specialized items can be sold as plans through publications catering to devotees of each interest. If there are already companies advertising plans for sale, it's a good sign that the market is receptive.

You could start by offering your ideas to existing publishers of plans, whether they are magazines or independent publishers. Write a letter telling them what you have available and ask if they are interested. Include information on your qualifications and a self-addressed stamped envelope (SASE) for their reply. Don't send the plans unless they express interest.

The other route is to sell them yourself through classified or display ads. The art of selling via direct mail has been exhaustively covered in many books. I've listed several in Resources (see p. 150). Start out small, always offer a money-back guarantee and treat your customers well and fairly. It takes time to build such a sideline but if you're a creative designer and a draftsman, you can have a nice kitchen-table business. Before you run ads, buy several different sets of plans from various advertisers to see how they put their packages together. Remember that it always pays to imitate and improve upon existing success.

WRITING ARTICLES AND BOOKS

Writing and selling how-to articles and books is a natural extension of professional woodworking if you have the ability to demonstrate and explain your skills to others clearly. There are at least 25 magazines and newsletters that cater to woodworkers. Add in other craft areas and the list is much longer. The basics steps to writing articles for money include:

▶ Research the publication that interests you. Read some back issues to get a feel for style and substance and to avoid duplicating areas they've covered recently. While you're researching, jot down ideas for articles similar to those you're reading. Be sure to read the shorter pieces and regular departments since these are often great places to break in.

▶ Write to the editor and ask for writer's guidelines. Always include a SASE for their reply. Most magazines receive dozens of letters daily and many will not reply unless you include a stamped envelope.

▶ Following their guidelines, write a brief (one page) query letter outlining your story idea. Include a catchy title, a quick blow-by-blow description of what you'll cover and your brief biography, including experience. You might include a sample article if you have one. List photos and illustrations you will provide and/or ones that will be required. Wait for a positive reply before writing the article.

▶ Send out a lot of queries at once but don't send the same idea to several editors. Known as multiple submissions, this activity is frowned upon and may put you in the position of angering an editor when another one wants the same story as the first. Once an idea is rejected, repackage it and send it out to another editor at a different magazine.

▶ If you get a positive response ask what rights the publisher buys, how much the publisher pays and when. The ideal is first North American rights and payment upon acceptance rather than publication. I don't recommend writing for free or giving away all your rights. Often these articles are sold in book form as anthologies, may appear on the Internet or in other formats. You should get paid for each use.

▶ Beat your deadlines, proofread your manuscript carefully, use standard manuscript format and include a diskette version if requested.

Selling articles is a great way to establish yourself as an expert, receive the gratification of seeing yourself in print and make a little money. Even more important, it can lead to writing books about woodworking, an interesting and rewarding way to earn some money while providing an interested audience with valuable information. Once you have some experience and a track record as a published writer/woodworker, you can use the same querying technique with the publishers of woodworking books.

▼▼▼

TEACHING

One of the fastest-growing segments of the woodworking business is schools and classes for woodworkers. Such opportunities might include continuing-education classes at night in a local high school's shop, two-week intensive sessions at specialized woodworking schools or full-time college-degree programs. Your skills and experience are valuable qualifications for teaching, and many part-time or instructor positions do not require teaching credentials.

Usually you can begin by offering a simple seminar or class through your local school system. Put together a course outline and present it to the continuing-education office or ask someone in the office how to go about it. You may need to show these people your portfolio and put together a resumé focusing on your woodworking background and any teaching or training experience you have.

While you probably won't get rich by teaching, you can develop relationships that will lead to commissions, find potential employees and build your reputation. In my area, a local college has a major crafts program, and many of the instructors are the first ones area architects turn to for woodworking projects. Their teaching credentials establish them as experts.

There is a trend toward woodworking schools that offer hands-on training for amateur woodworkers combined with the opportunity to work in a large shop under expert supervision. Setting up such a school can offer a nice source of income, however it is vital to consider the liability exposure you have when inexperienced people work in your shop. Adequate insurance and legal advice are essential before starting a teaching venture.

For more about teaching as a profit center see the profile of Paul and Bonnie Rung on pp. 85-86.

SELLING YOUR DESIGN SKILLS

A major part of your education as a woodworker is learning to design the pieces you build. Design skill is a complex mixture of art, craft and problem-solving ability. Often you will be expected to do design work as part of your bids, and you should charge for it. Design work can become a lucrative profit center.

There are many specialist design areas including kitchen design, furniture design, design for manufacture and construction detailing for architects and interior designers. If you have developed a specialty in one of these disciplines, there is no reason why you should not promote it for its own sake.

SELLING ITEMS MADE BY OTHER CRAFTSPEOPLE

Occasionally you may find another woodworker or craftsperson whose work meshes with your own in a mutually beneficial manner, which may represent an opportunity to offer your customers additional products and services without doing additional labor. If you have a shop or showroom why not take other craftspeople's work on a consignment basis, taking a markup for yourself when you sell their work?

I covered outsourcing in detail in Chapter 11, so keep it in mind as a way to enhance your earnings. Another excellent way to work with fellow craftspeople is through a cooperative shop or gallery.

SHOWROOMS, GALLERIES AND SHOPS

To have a showroom, shop or gallery is a major business decision because these are, in essence, retail businesses that require a lot of money, time and effort. You may find it worth your while to put together a display area in your shop or to build a sample chest that you can take to meetings with customers. Often this kind of introduction to retailing is the first step to opening a shop or gallery if you find you enjoy this kind of business.

Many areas of the country have cooperative crafts galleries that are owned and run by groups of craftspeople who share the duties while providing themselves with a regular place to show their work. These co-ops can work if they are well-managed and if everyone does his or her share. It is like taking on a large number of partners, so make sure you can extricate yourself if things don't work out. Also it is important to look at the mix of styles and pieces to ensure that your work stands out and is not too similar to another participating woodworker.

These co-ops are good ways to get involved in your locality's craft community and to learn about the gallery scene. Artists are always willing to share, and you can pick up a lot of useful information by joining a group. You also share the expense of advertising, publicity, openings, overhead and staffing, so make sure everything is spelled out in writing before you join.

Again, showing your work with others can lead to commissions from fellow artists and opportunities to swap work or make and get referrals, which are valuable benefits. And, as a group member, you may get more exposure than you would as a lone wolf. The down side, of course, is that if the work of your fellow members is substandard your work can be dragged down with it. Take a good look at the whole package.

There are many opportunities for you to use your woodworking skills profitably. Every day I pick up a trade magazine and read about another woodworker with an unusual specialty or product line. It's a big world, and that means that an idea working well on one side of the country may work just as well on the other. Sometimes you can adapt another shop's idea to your own situation and end up with your own profit center. Once you develop the attitude that spots opportunity, you'll find many ways to enhance your woodworking business success.

THE FUTURE

This final chapter is about change and the future of your woodworking business. Even the smallest business can benefit immeasurably from a regular reevaluation of its goals and motivations. Probably the number one reason for small-business success and longevity is the overall vision of the owner. Without some kind of bigger picture you'll be stuck in a common self-employment rut: Always fighting to survive while losing the original spark of enthusiasm that got you started in the first place.

There is a cycle that many small-business owners experience during their first few years of operation. They start out full of enthusiasm and energy. They're thrilled by the opportunity to create their own working life, free from bosses and boredom. They plunge in and pour their hearts and souls into the business.

Eventually, they hit a wall from long days and coping with too many new or confusing commissions and tasks. They had the woodworking skills but now they're dealing with the accounting, selling, managing, collecting and buying skills. It may seem that they're doing less woodworking and more business managing. Eventually they become disenchanted and consider going back to work for someone else, downsizing or selling their business. This is the low point, and the place where it is hardest to know what to do.

It is at that point where choices become limited. To avoid this uncomfortable scenario, you must consider the future of your business now, at the start, or when things are going well. In this chapter I'm going to look at "vision" and ways you can integrate the future into your present-day work life.

A BUSINESS IS A SYSTEM

Your shop and skills are part of a system that designs, fabricates and sells woodworking services and products for your customers. One of the keys to long-term business success is to use this concept constantly to improve and upgrade the system you've created. This constant fine-tuning will enable you to produce better work with less effort, offer more competitive prices while retaining quality and offer your customers a consistently reliable product or service that they will use repeatedly.

The advantages of any systems approach over a random method are:

▶ You don't reinvent the wheel every time you have a new task to perform. When you learn something useful you incorporate it into your system so that you don't repeat your old mistakes.

▶ You can teach a system to someone else. The ideal business is one that can be easily taught to others without requiring extremely specialized skills or large amounts of experience. By developing and understanding the systems you use, you can show others how to operate them based on your experience. This becomes a major advantage when hiring employees or selling your business.

▶ A tested system saves time and money. Instead of randomly attacking tasks as they scream for attention, you have a plan for a step-by-step approach. You can set aside the right amount of time, set up your tools, assemble your supplies and complete a task, knowing exactly what you'll be doing next week or next month.

▶ The systems approach applies to more than woodworking. It's a way to get referrals, for instance, and no matter how simple, it will generate more referrals than a scattershot approach. So many calls and mailings per week, an automatic request for referrals upon completion of every job and an incentive system that you always honor promptly can mean business success that grows gradually, step by step.

▶ Having a system makes unpleasant or unfamiliar tasks much easier. If you are uncomfortable with selling, you can develop a simple method for handling sales and use it regularly without variation. Eventually the system and your subconscious will take over and sales will no longer be something you dread.

The only way to create an effective system for your shop is to have an end in mind. This end will be the result of running your system. With a set of goals for your life and business, you will have a target to work toward. The processes you set up for your business will determine whether you reach your goals.

▼▼▼

GOALS FOR THE FUTURE

Many professional woodworkers I work with often complain that they would like to go in every day and work without having to deal with the issues covered in this book. I ask them to consider this: Why not get a job somewhere if putting in your eight hours is the goal? The answer of course is that their goal is not to work for someone else. Often, people want freedom, power to make decisions, control over their time and other similar goals. At least this is what gets them started in business. It's when they lose track of these goals that they get frustrated and feel they've lost control.

Write down the reasons you want to be in business for yourself and where you'd like to be five years from now. Be specific and don't worry if what you want seems like a fantasy. Setting your targets too low means you'll always be dragging your feet. Perhaps you'd like to develop a product line based on your own designs, or build historic-reproduction furniture or have a one-person show of your art furniture. These goals are totally realistic. Other people just like you realize them every day, because they knew what they wanted.

Your goals may be income related. Perhaps you have a specific figure you want to make per year or an amount you need for retirement. Look at what you do now. Can you attain that salary doing what you do now? Are you putting aside enough? What kinds of changes can you make that will increase your income or the value of your business?

To reach your goals, think in terms of the systems your business uses and how they can be improved, adapted or changed. Perhaps you would like to sell your business five years from now. If you are a one-person custom furniture shop, all you'll have to sell is a roomful of used tools. You need to build up your business and create a moneymaking machine that another person can take over and run profitably without your presence. Only then can you sell your shop.

SELLING YOUR COMPANY

Because selling your business is a good example of how a systems approach can increase the value of your work, I'm going to look at it in more detail. Even if you think you wouldn't want to sell your business, the systems approach is worth considering because it can be used to improve any woodshop.

Let's say that Joe is in his fifties and decides he wants to sell his small woodworking business within the next five years. He has a small cabinet shop with three employees who build custom cabinetry for business and residential use. His work comes from bidding, personal connections and some advertising. Basically he gets most of his work from a small network of longtime customers. Everything he does is custom, meaning that is it is built to specifications that differ from job to job.

At this point Joe's business is not worth much because it is totally dependent on Joe for its customers, planning, organization and a lot of the actual woodworking skill. His employees do a lot of grunt work, and he has a high turnover and trouble finding good workers. He has also learned that he can't delegate work to others because "if he wants it done right, he has to do it himself."

To make his business salable, Joe needs a major shift in perspective, and he gets it when he has a business broker value his company. The price he is given is low. He can't believe that this is what he has to show for working so hard for the past 10 years. The broker explains that service businesses with hands-on owners aren't worth much because it is too hard for the owner to pass on his special knowledge to a new owner. The systems are in Joe's head rather than out on the shop floor.

Joe has two choices: Keep working and try to save as much money as possible for retirement and just close the doors when the time comes, or change his business methods with the specific goal of increasing its value. After thinking things over, he realizes that he is going to work for five more years at least so why not improve the business? Either way, he'll still be working in his shop.

Joe goes to his local Small Business Administration office and they hook him up with a mentor from SCORE, the Service Corps of Retired Executives. He also takes some business courses at the local university and starts picking the teacher's brain after class. He does a lot of reading and starts to understand that he has just been surviving rather than thriving. He also learns what makes a business valuable to a buyer.

Profits are a major feature of a selling price. The buyer wants a good return on the investment, and profits are the return. Cash flow is also important because an uneven cash flow requires a large amount of operating capital (cash on hand) to keep things running while waiting for income. And, most important for a small company like Joe's, there must be systems that the new owner can learn and operate without too much specialized knowledge.

The prime example of this approach is the McDonald's restaurant chain. Joe's management class visits one, and his professor has them look at the systems that make McDonald's so valuable. It is a machine for making food that is consistent, fresh and hot all the time. It is also a machine that can be run by one manager and a bunch of high school students while generating millions in annual sales.

While Joe has no desire to turn his shop into the McDonald's of cabinet shops, he realizes that there are many changes he can make over five years to add value to his company. He and his wife hammer out an action plan with the specific goal of making his company worth a certain price. He writes down a specific figure for the selling price.

Joe will do the following:

▶ He will create a profile of his customers and look for additional products and services that they need and he can offer them. He will start making all of his business decisions based on his customers' needs rather than on his own interests. In fact, he will make the interests of his customers into his interests.

▶ He will look at the entire process he uses on each job, from first contact to completion, and write it down. Once he has written out the process(es), he will look for ways to automate as many as possible. This means small changes such as automatically entering the customer into his database and important changes such as maintaining a regular schedule of contacts and updates to keep his customers informed at every stage of their project.

▶ He will look at the products he makes and sells and look for ways to save money and time by outsourcing some items while focusing his employees on developing certain skills that are most profitable. For instance, he decides to purchase all his standard cabinet boxes from a factory and focus on training his employees to do custom doors and finishes.

▶ He documents these processes and trains his employees to follow a checklist at each stage of a project so that they always know what they're doing next, how long it should take and, just as important, why each task is necessary.

▶ He develops a simple incentive plan for his employees that rewards them with bonuses based on growth and profitability. He also trains each of them to answer the phones consistently, to treat customers like royalty and to look for opportunities to sell the company's services.

▶ He documents his system in a journal that he develops into an operating manual for his business. When he sells it he'll be able to train the new owner, using his systems and operating manual, to run the shop profitably. In essence, he is making himself dispensable and transferring his skill and experience to the company.

This process is no different from setting up a jig to produce multiple parts for a furniture project. Joe is creating "jigs" to help him run his business. And guess what? Joe starts enjoying his work more. He spends less time overseeing everyone every minute of the day. He attracts better workers who have a stake in their own success. At the end of the five years he probably won't sell because he enjoys his work, makes more money than ever and can actually take a day off once in while. And if he wants to sell, he won't have to look far. His company's enhanced reputation and profitability will have made it a desirable commodity, worth far more than the value of the tools in the shop.

This approach to managing your small woodworking business may seem cold and technical to some but ultimately it can mean both monetary and psychological success. Even the small basement shop cranking out crafts for a summer show circuit can benefit from a systems-oriented approach. Most of us use systems but don't consciously work on them. Your enjoyment of the business of woodworking can be greatly enhanced by taking a look at the big picture of what you really want and designing a machine to achieve it. Think of it as a furniture design you've refined and fine-tuned until it is a classic that will sell for years to come.

Reading books like this is the first step to learning the ways that successful professional woodworkers make a good living doing something they love. The *profits* in *Profitable Woodworking* are far more than dollars and cents. They are a sense of accomplishment, pride in your craftsmanship, the fun of interacting with other skilled people from all walks of life and the creation of enduring articles that function well, look beautiful and delight the senses in a way that only wood can.

RESOURCES

GENERAL BUSINESS

Gerber, Michael. *The E-Myth.* New York: Harper Business, 1986. *Insight into the reasons why businesses fail and a system for avoiding failure. Important reading for those who are leaving the nine-to-five world and starting out on their own.*

Hawken, Paul. *Growing a Business.* New York: Simon & Schuster, 1988. *One of the best books out there for anyone starting a business. Entertaining and realistic. Highly recommended.*

GENERAL MARKETING HELP

Bangs, David H., Jr. *Business Planning Guide.* Dover, N.H.: Upstart Publishing Co., 1982.

Bangs, David H., Jr. *Market Planning Guide.* Dover, N.H.: Upstart Publishing Co., 1994. *Excellent nuts-and-bolts, small-business-oriented guides to using business and marketing plans.*

Levinson, Jay Conrad. *Guerrilla Marketing.* Boston: Houghton-Mifflin Co., 1984.

Levinson, Jay Conrad. *Guerrilla Marketing Attack.* Boston: Houghton-Mifflin Co., 1989. *Jay Conrad Levinson's* Guerrilla *series is the definitive general small-business marketing tool. The series is based on the premise that a creative small-business marketer can beat out competition big and small by being innovative.*

ACCOUNTING

Kamaroff, Bernard. *Small-Time Operator.* Laytonville, Calif.: Bell Springs Publishing, 1992. *Understanding cash flow, billing, profits and the way money flows through your business is vital to making marketing decisions. Small-Time Operator is a classic how-to book for small-business accounting. Use Kamaroff's knowledge to learn to talk to your accountant (and save money!).*

SALES

Gallagher, Bill, Orvel Ray Wilson and Jay Conrad Levinson. *Guerrilla Selling.* Boston: Houghton-Mifflin, 1992. *Another* Guerrilla *book with a good, though often idealized, approach to sales.*

ADVERTISING

Bruneau, Edmund A. *Rx (Prescription) for Advertising.* Spokane, Wash.: Boston Books, 1986. *The book for the business owner considering the use of advertising. How to deal with writers, artists, agencies, media, etc., in a down-to-earth voice.*

WOODWORKING BUSINESS

Edic, Martin. *The Woodworker's Marketing Guide.* Newtown, Conn.: The Taunton Press, 1995. *How to connect with the people who buy and recommend your work.*

Tolpin, Jim. *Working at Woodworking.* Newtown, Conn.: The Taunton Press, 1991. *A glimpse into the professional woodworking life written by an active woodworker.*

MAGAZINES AND PERIODICALS

American Craft. New York: The American Craft Council. *An invaluable resource for show schedules, gallery information and the names of people in the craft world who can help you sell your work and build a reputation.*

Architectural Record. New York: McGraw-Hill. *This expensive, glossy magazine is worth picking up to catch a glimpse into the world of commercial and residential architecture. Not only will you pick up on trends, you may find places where you can market your woodworking services.*

CabinetMaker. Chicago: Delta Communications. *Aimed more at large shops but valuable for its resource sections, shop profiles and annual buying guide. You may be able to get a free subscription by writing to them on your company letterhead.*

Custom Woodworking Business. Lincolnshire, Ill.: Vance Publishing Corp. *A glossy trade aimed at small and medium shops.*

Fine Homebuilding. Newtown, Conn.: The Taunton Press. *As a pro, your work will often be integrated into new construction and renovation projects. For that reason, you can't afford not to read* Fine Homebuilding *along with* Fine Woodworking.

Fine Woodworking. Newtown, Conn.: The Taunton Press. *The classic magazine for skilled amateurs and pros.*

Home Furniture. Newtown, Conn.: The Taunton Press. *A quarterly look at what your contemporaries are building and selling. Includes design articles and advertising from other woodworkers.*

Inc. Magazine. Boston: Goldhirsh Group. *A source of useful tips and advice from your peers. As with any of these resources, even one small but profitable idea easily justifies the price of a subscription or book.*

Interior Design. New York: Cahners Publishing Co. *The magazine of the professional design world, including both residential and commercial design. An excellent source of names, resources and information on trends and the needs of the large corporate market for woodworking.*

Wood & Wood Products. Lincolnshire, Ill.: Vance Publishing Corp. *The trade magazine for big manufacturers. It may be worth a subscription for the annual supplier's resource guide, an excellent reference for finding anything from drawer pulls to TV elevators to Euro cabinets. When your architect specifies something weird, this the place to find it and look like a hero.*

Woodshop News. Essex, Conn.: Soundings Publications. *A tabloid-size newsprint trade magazine for the professional woodworking business. Good for its profiles of other woodworkers, sources for supplies and informative articles about the business of woodworking.*

MISCELLANEOUS

The Small Business Administration (SBA). *Check your phone book under Federal Government to find the nearest office. SBA has many useful, free publications, can offer help with planning and financing, and can hook you up with the Service Corps of Retired Executives (SCORE).*

Modern Postcard, 6354 Corte del Abeto #E, Carlsbad, CA 92009. *Great prices and quality for color postcards and flyers.*

ABC Pictures, Inc. 1867 East Florida Street, Springfield, MO 65803-4583. *This company can produce 8x10 black-and-white glossies of your work in large quantities inexpensively.*

INDEX

PUBLISHER: JAMES P. CHIAVELLI

ACQUISITIONS EDITOR: RICK PETERS

PUBLISHING COORDINATOR: JOANNE RENNA

EDITOR: SALLY SMITH

COPY/PRODUCTION EDITOR: DIANE SINITSKY

LAYOUT ARTIST: ROSALIE VACCARO

TYPEFACE: GARAMOND

PAPER: SOMERSET MATTE, 70 LB.

PRINTER: BAWDEN PRINTING, ELDRIDGE, IOWA